Tenaha

Corruption and Cover-up in Small Town Texas

Stewart Fillmore

ISBN:1547248947
ISBN-13:9781547248940

DEDICATION

To my wife Jena,

We were just kids when I started with the FBI and you supported me all the way. From helping me train for Quantico, move to the frozen tundra of Chicago, to my farewell luncheon. For living with the frustration of not knowing what I was working on. Very simply, nothing else would have much meaning without you there to have shared it. We aren't perfect but we've perfectly made our way together. Thank you from the bottom of my heart.

————

A special thanks to my fellow "street" Agents and Field Office support personnel. You are the core of the FBI. Your great work, commitment, and loyalty to our country are largely unsung. It was an honor, a privilege and a lot of fun to have served with you.

CONTENTS

INTRODUCTION

"Fred better come up with some more cash for me and my family or his fat ass is gonna be up in here with me."

These were the threatening words of a man in jail frustrated at the lack of money his wife was getting from a criminal associate enjoying life outside jail. The man, Roderrete "Rod" McClure, was serving a 36 month federal prison sentence after pleading guilty to being a felon in possession of a firearm.

The man McClure referred to was Fred Walker, his cousin and the former City Marshal of Tenaha, Texas. McClure was still facing federal narcotics trafficking charges, which meant the possibility of significantly more prison time. Being the only one in jail was frustrating — but potentially lucrative for McClure. Most people don't go to jail with the thought of making money, but Rod McClure is not like most people.

McClure was in jail largely by his own choice. He was given multiple chances to cooperate and help himself. Fifteen years earlier, he had been an eager DEA informant. One of his former DEA handlers said "McClure would have informed on his mother if it helped him out of a jam." A year and a half earlier, McClure was an anonymous source for both a CNN story and a federal civil lawsuit alleging civil rights violations against a District Attorney, a Mayor, and three law enforcement officials. Now he was in jail, mad and frustrated at a man McClure knew was the main subject of an FBI corruption investigation. And despite his anger, McClure refused to cooperate against Walker.

Maybe McClure had changed from his informant days. Maybe he wouldn't actually inform on a family member to help himself. Or maybe he was afraid of something Walker could reveal — something McClure felt was better left unsaid — even if it meant languishing in jail while Walker enjoyed freedom. But the narcotics charges McClure was facing carried potential penalties of over 25 years. Apparently keeping Walker silent was worth gambling on 25 years in prison to McClure. The strange death of a local meth cook whose home was raided for child pornography by the Secret Service may have been what needed to be kept quiet.

Life in small town East Texas can be idyllic. Everyone knows each other. Parades, festivals and Friday night high school football games are a part of life. It's quiet and peaceful and time moves a little slower than in a big city.

Tenaha (pronounced Ten-uh-haw) is no different.

It sits in Shelby County, one of the oldest counties in Texas and has a population of just over 1,000. Although the downtown area has seen better days, there is a modern, well-equipped football stadium to watch the Tenaha Tigers play football on cool Friday nights each fall. Many of the residents have lived there for generations. Old time Country and Western star Tex Ritter, who was born just up the road in Carthage, Texas, memorialized the place in the folk song, "Tenaha, Timpson, Bobo, and Blair."

Unfortunately real life doesn't always fit quaintly into the stanzas of a happy song, and though on the surface things appeared to be like the mythical Mayberry, there was a rotten underbelly to the small town.

Tenaha came to national attention in 2009 after a segment of the CNN show "Anderson Cooper 360" highlighted a number of money seizures made during car stops by the local City Marshal's Office — and the lack of associated prosecutions by the District Attorney. The segment followed a 2008 federal civil lawsuit, *Morrow vs. City of Tenaha, et al.*, filed by several individuals who were stopped by local and county law enforcement and claimed to be victims of racism and profiling. The lawsuit alleged that money and personal property seized in the car stops was extorted from the victims by the Tenaha cops in exchange for not going to jail or under the threat of losing custody of their children.

The CNN segment caught the attention of the United States Department of Justice, the Texas Attorney General's Office, the FBI and the Texas Rangers, the legendary investigative agency of the Texas Department of Public Safety. A criminal investigation with the involvement of each agency was started and based on the allegations; it was certainly an appropriate response for the highest levels of law enforcement.

But just as the real life Tenaha wasn't like the Tex Ritter song, the facts alleged in *Morrow* weren't as clear cut and incriminating as presented in the Anderson Cooper segment.

The federal investigation revealed the TV segment just scratched the surface of what was going on in Tenaha. The true facts were deeper and began appearing only after a failed extortion scheme carried out by someone calling himself Jack Frost came to light.

Along with the Jack Frost extortion scheme, a series of threatening letters were mailed to several local churches and businesses in Tenaha. The letters were aimed at Deputy City Marshal Barry Washington, an officer highlighted in the CNN segment for his part in the controversial car stops. The letters contained vile, racist and threatening language and images, and appeared to be aimed at intimidating Washington into leaving town.

Washington was also a defendant in the Morrow civil case and a subject of the federal investigation. He was definitely the eye of the storm in Tenaha.

A retired Texas state trooper with a well known reputation for narcotics interdiction, Washington's presence in Tenaha rocked the status quo and his seizures of large amounts of money and drugs brought a lot of attention that some in town didn't want.

So sets the stage for a story of corruption, extortion, drugs, guns, illegal wiretapping and possibly murder in a small town deep in the beautiful piney woods of East Texas.

1

HOW DID I END UP IN TENAHA?

You're now far more aware of what was happening in Tenaha, Texas than I was when the case was assigned to me in April 2009. I didn't know where it was and I can't say now if I remember ever hearing of it prior to working this case. For such a small town, it is unbelievable how much criminal activity was going on there. Before I go into the story though, I'll briefly give you some background on myself, my experience in the FBI and how corruption cases are worked.

My exposure to the FBI came early in life. The doctor who delivered me was named J. Edgar Jones. But my first doctor having a name similar to J. Edgar Hoover, the longtime Director of the FBI, was just the first signpost of what lay ahead for me. My grandfather, John E. Franklin, was an FBI Special Agent from May 1941 until he retired in September 1962.

He was initially assigned to the Philadelphia Field Office for a short time before being moved to the Reading, Pennsylvania Resident Agency. After a brief time in Reading, he was transferred to the Detroit Field Office in 1942 where he was assigned to investigate German espionage.

With World War II raging, one of the most important priorities of the FBI was catching German spies and saboteurs. One such case my grandfather worked on involved a spy ring headed by a French Canadian countess named Grace Buchanan-Dineen.

In a press release from the FBI in August 1943, Buchanan-Dineen is described as an "attractive, well-educated descendant of French nobility carefully trained by Germany in espionage work."

She had been recruited and trained by the Nazis in Hungary and entered the United States in 1941 before the attack on Pearl Harbor. After settling in Detroit, Buchanan-Dineen recruited several individuals with Nazi sympathies to gather intelligence about production and movement of war materials, location of war production plants and movement of troops and high ranking military personnel.

The FBI intercepted a letter sent by Buchanan-Dineen to a New York address known to be connected with Nazi spying activity. As a result of being caught, Buchanan-Dineen began cooperating and she participated in counter-espionage by transmitting false information back to her German handlers — under the supervision of the FBI in coordination with military intelligence services.

One of Buchanan-Dineen's co-conspirators was Dr. Fred W. Thomas, a Detroit surgeon and member of the German-American Bund, an American Nazi organization. My grandfather arrested and interrogated Thomas and later testified at his trial where he was convicted and sentenced to 16 years in prison.

In an annual performance review, my grandfather was commended for his work on the Buchanan-Dineen case. The supervisor wrote "Special Agent Franklin functioned extremely well and displayed considerable ingenuity and skill in interrogation." This assignment on what would have been a high priority case for an Agent with a little over a year of investigative experience certainly speaks to the confidence his superiors had in him.

Shortly after the end of the war in 1945 however, my grandfather resigned from the FBI. He planned to make his riches as a salesman for a toy manufacturing company in Detroit. But selling toys didn't turn out to be as lucrative as he thought and I doubt it held much excitement compared to catching German spies. In 1947, he wrote a personal letter to Director Hoover and requested reinstatement.

Hoover welcomed him back in and assigned him to the Houston Field Office in the one-man Galveston Resident Agency.

There are 56 FBI field offices centrally located throughout the United States and Puerto Rico. Within each field office, which are also called Divisions, there are smaller satellite offices called Resident Agencies, known within the FBI as RAs. RAs vary in size primarily depending on the population of the territory covered. The assigned territory is generally made up of a number of counties.

In the days before Las Vegas became a gambling Mecca, the island city known as "The Free State of Galveston" was a gambling destination with clubs that drew the likes of Frank Sinatra, Tony Bennett and other big stars of that era.

The Galveston gambling clubs weren't legal but were tolerated by the local population because of the tourist money that flowed into the city. My grandfather conducted surveillances and gathered intelligence on the clubs, but being in a one-man office, there was only so much he could do, especially with the friendly attitude that the local politicians and judges held toward the illegal — but prosperous — local industry.

I'd like to say I heard the stories I'm telling you about my grandfather's service in the FBI directly from him as I was growing up but he died when I was too young to know him. I have a vague memory of him as kind of a funny guy who smoked a cigar. So I grew up knowing that he had been in the FBI but I didn't know any specifics about his career.

A few years ago I got his personnel file from the Bureau through a Freedom of Information request. It was very detailed and contained information about his initial background investigation including his references.

One of his references was Alfred P. Murrah, who was a Federal Judge in Oklahoma at the time my grandfather came into the FBI. If that name sounds familiar, the federal building in Oklahoma City that was bombed by Timothy McVeigh in 1995 was named after Judge Murrah.

Prior to the FBI, my grandfather was the Chief Federal Probation Officer for the Eastern District of Oklahoma and worked with Judge Murrah. I later worked a small portion of the OKBOMB case, as the investigation of the Murrah building bombing was called in the FBI. It was a small coincidence in my career but not the last.

It was fascinating going through my grandfather's file. One thing I noticed were the forms used, style of writing, and overall documentation were almost the same as they were when I came into the FBI over 40 years later.

There were numerous letters from Director Hoover — many of them letters of commendation and a few letters of censure. One of the letters of censure resulted after my grandfather; while still a relatively new agent, failed to properly inventory the required necessities of his assigned Bureau car — flashlight, first aid kit, spare tire, etc.

Director Hoover kept a tight control on the Bureau and practically managed the day to day operations personally — down to some of the tiniest details. One funny Hoover letter in the file, although it probably wasn't funny for one of my grandfather's fellow Agents assigned up the Gulf Coast from Galveston in Port Arthur, involved the aftermath of Hurricane Carla in 1961.

The letter was addressed to both my grandfather and the Port Arthur Agent (whose name was redacted from my copy of the file). Director Hoover excoriated the Port Arthur Agent and showered praise on my grandfather for their actions during the hurricane. My grandfather had manned the Galveston FBI office which was located on the fifth floor of the Post Office Building near downtown during the hurricane. The Port Arthur Agent evacuated inland and left his office unmanned.

In a follow up letter from the Port Arthur Agent defending his actions, he explained that the Civil Defense had ordered a general evacuation. Unfortunately I don't have the original letter, but there was a handwritten notation from Director Hoover — which would have no doubt been in blue ink as he was the only person in the FBI who could write in blue ink — that said "Since when do we take orders from Civil Defense?"

The file wasn't specific about what Hoover expected my grandfather and the other Agent to do. Most likely he wanted the offices manned to prevent looters from stealing FBI files and equipment. Mr. Hoover took the protection of FBI files very seriously and apparently didn't mind risking the personal safety of his Agents to ensure it.

As I said earlier I knew my grandfather had been an FBI Agent but it wasn't something that I grew up thinking I would like to do. As a young man however, I did like reading about the gangsters of the 1930s like John Dillinger, Pretty Boy Floyd and Baby Face Nelson, and how the FBI tracked them all down.

Baby Face Nelson actually killed three FBI Agents, in two separate gun battles, and has the infamous distinction of being the person who has killed the most FBI Agents.

—

My impression of the FBI was largely drawn from the image that was created back in the 1930s. Beyond a general interest though an FBI career was not something I set out to do.

I had an otherwise normal childhood growing up in Tyler, Texas, where I was an avid tennis player through high school. If I gave much thought to a career in those formative years it would have been more dreams of being the next Jimmy Connors than the next Melvin Purvis, the FBI Agent who chased down Dillinger and Pretty Boy Floyd.

So when I pursued a degree in accounting at the University of Texas at Tyler, it was only because a school counselor suggested it would be an area of study that would lead to a good job. I wasn't aware at that time the FBI primarily hired lawyers and accountants as Special Agents, another coincidence that worked in my favor.

Although accounting was not something I particularly liked or had any special talent for, I muscled my way to good grades and found it had one aspect that was a natural fit for me — there was an element of puzzle solving to it. I love solving puzzles of almost any kind — crosswords, sudokus, word jumbles, cryptoquotes, etc. I didn't know it at the time, but my enjoyment of puzzles would later be a great asset for me (pun intended as an accounting major) in the FBI.

So in another coincidence, just before graduation, I learned of an opening at the Dallas Field Office for a position artfully known as an Accounting Technician. It was a support position that assisted Special Agents in investigating financial crimes, generally known as white collar crime.

I applied for the job and after a thorough background investigation, just like the one my grandfather had gone through before me that looks into previous employment, friends, references, places lived, checks for previous arrests and credit checks, I was hired in August 1987.

It just so happened at the time, the FBI was heavily involved investigating the savings and loan crisis, a national meltdown of the thrift industry that was centered in Texas. I looked through and analyzed thousands of pages of loan documents, served subpoenas at banks and other businesses and helped prepare for and assisted in several trials.

It was not a typical accounting job and that was fine with me. Although I was still not sold on a career in the FBI, I surely thought it would be something cool to do for the time being. However as I continued in the support position, I grew to really like my fellow FBI employees and felt a special camaraderie.

I became good friends with several Special Agents and they encouraged me to apply for the position. To make myself competitive, I studied for and passed the CPA exam in my first sitting. I also began studying for the entrance exam for graduate school.

In the fall of 1989, I took the written test for the Special Agent position. I was told it was more of a psychological test and there was not really a way to study for it. However there was another test that would be administered before the written exam that I was able to prepare for: Each applicant had to be able to pull the trigger of a "red-handled revolver" 50 times in each hand.

The "red handle" was a real revolver used in training that was permanently disabled from firing but otherwise fully operational. The purpose of the 50 pull test was to assess the hand strength of applicants to ensure they could handle the rigorous firearms training involved in becoming an FBI Special Agent. It may sound easy but it is more difficult than it might initially seem. I practiced by using a hand strengthener. And believe it or not, the 50 pull test was also a way of letting applicants know that as an FBI Agent, you are required to carry a firearm. I was surprised to learn how many people who applied to be an FBI Special Agent didn't realize they would have to carry a gun.

After passing the written exam and the 50 trigger pull test, I next sat for an interview. I was sent to the Houston Field Office for the interview because I already worked in Dallas and knew almost everyone in the office. The interview was conducted by three veteran Special Agents. Although I was friends with several Special Agents, the interview was still an intimidating process.

I recall coming out of the interview feeling that I had not done very well. About a month later however, in December 1989, I received the results and learned I passed the interview.

Pending an updated background investigation I would be assigned to a training class at the FBI Academy located in Quantico, Virginia. The academy actually sits, in a separate facility, on the grounds of the Marine Corps Base Quantico which is where Marine Officers are trained.

While I waited for a training class, I began physically training to be prepared for a fitness test that would be administered on Day 1, which included a two-mile run, push-ups, sit-ups, pull-ups, and a short sprint involving agility that was called a shuttle run. Although I had already passed both a medical exam and a reduced version of the Quantico fitness test as part of the application process, I wanted to make sure I could meet the rigorous standards for each event.

—

In June 1990, I packed my bags and traveled to the FBI Academy for 16 weeks of New Agent Training, or NAT. The NAT would include firearms training, classroom instruction, physical fitness requirements and defensive tactics training.

In firearms training, we were instructed in the use of the Smith & Wesson Model 13 .357 revolver, the Remington 870 .12 gauge shotgun, and the Heckler & Koch MP5 9mm semi-automatic rifle. We shot hundreds of rounds with each weapon, although the revolver was considered our primary weapon.

We were taught the basics of marksmanship and how to shoot in various stances while standing, kneeling and prone from distances of up to 50 yards. I always enjoyed the firearms training and was relatively good at it — although

I wasn't even close to being the top shooter in my class.

The most stress I remember regarding firearms came after we finished shooting and it was time to clean our guns.

The instructors were very strict regarding the procedure for cleaning a weapon. They kept a close eye on us in the cleaning room. They randomly inspected our guns to ensure they were properly cleaned and I recall the instructors always finding something that needed more attention. To this day, I'm somewhat picky in making sure my gun is properly and thoroughly clean.

I will point out that my training class was the last in FBI history to be issued revolvers. The transition to semi-automatic pistols which hold more than twice the number of bullets of a six-shot revolver occurred as a result of a tragic shootout in Miami in 1986 between eight FBI Agents and two violent bank robbers.

Although the FBI Agents outnumbered the suspects 4-to-1, they were outgunned by one of them, who wielded a semi-automatic rifle. Two of the Miami FBI Agents were killed and five severely wounded before both of the suspects were killed. A study conducted after the shootout recommended a change to semi-automatic pistols because of their larger capacity magazines. It took four years to implement the transition at the Academy. I carried a revolver until 1993 when I transitioned to a semi-automatic pistol.

The classroom instruction covered legal topics, investigative techniques, ethics, informant development and interview and interrogation. The legal topics were primarily related to the requirements and standards for obtaining search and arrest warrants, Title III (wiretap) orders and other court orders. There was instruction on writing affidavits and investigative reports documenting investigative findings.

We learned what constituted probable cause, the standard by which search warrants are approved by judges. The classes were taught by veteran Agents who had spent years in the field and supplemented the instruction with real life stories that bolstered the academic work. We learned the value of informants and cooperating witnesses — individuals who were on the fringes of and in some cases involved in illegal activity who could provide real time insight into ongoing criminal schemes.

In addition to the firearms and classroom training, we also did intense strength and cardiovascular training. As I mentioned earlier I did my own training prior to arriving at the academy and scored toward the top of my class in overall fitness after the first fit test. There were some in my class, however, who didn't do as well as our instructors wanted them to do. So the entire class was subjected to a form of interval training that I best could describe as being close to a type of CrossFit training. And we did this training every day.

When our next fit test came around (there were three tests conducted over the course of the NAT), I actually did worse than I had done on the first test. After the second test, the instructors eased up on us and the required training was relaxed. I went back to the training I had done on my own, which was nothing special but was based on resting every other day to allow recovery. It worked for me because the third fit test score was my best of the three.

Another part of the physical training included an important aspect known as Defensive Tactics. This involved learning how to restrain individuals with handcuffs or other holds if necessary depending on the compliance of the suspect. This training to me was similar to basic martial arts training. We learned to fall properly, defend from someone attempting to steal our gun and the proper way to put handcuffs on a person. There are numerous techniques, depending on whether there is a compliant subject or a subject who is non-compliant, i.e. fighting back, to get handcuffs on them.

I know my instructors were very capable and adept at what they taught and I know that people perform under pressure the way they have practiced. But I must say that after I left the FBI Academy I was involved in numerous arrests of non-compliant subjects and those techniques taught under the academic setting at the Academy went out the window — I simply got the handcuffs on any way possible.

Toward the end of my training at the FBI Academy, we carried out several types of mock investigations at Hogan's Alley, a training facility that has the appearance of a small town. There is a bank, hotel, barber shop, pool hall, row homes, shops and a movie theater called The Biograph, the name of the theater in Chicago where gangster John Dillinger was killed by FBI Agents in 1934.

Hogan's Alley allows new Agents to train in a realistic setting to practice interviewing witnesses, conducting arrests and executing search warrants under a variety of scenarios. Role players are used as witnesses, victims, suspects and arrestees. New Agents are broken up into small teams, with one person being named a Team Leader who will assign various tasks to be carried out in each scenario.

For example, the team is given a brief set of facts: a bank robbery has occurred, a very minimal description of the suspect and/or a vehicle, and witnesses are present inside the bank. The Team Leader will assign part of the team to interview the witnesses and secure any evidence at the bank and part of the team to begin looking for the suspect or the vehicle. When the witnesses are interviewed, more clues and information become available and this is passed along to Agents looking for the suspect. Eventually the suspect is found in a house or other building and then an arrest is carried out. At the end of the training scenario, instructors give critiques in after-action meetings and point out things done correctly and incorrectly.

It was eye opening to me how real the training scenarios felt, from the time it started until it played out to a logical conclusion. In one situation simulating the execution of an arrest warrant for a violent subject, I was assigned to cover the rear exit of a house while entry was made in the front.

I was carrying a training shotgun and a training revolver, both of which were loaded with blanks. We drove up to the house, quickly got out and took up our assigned positions. I went to the back of the house and took cover behind a tree and focused on the back door. The entry team knocked loudly and yelled "FBI — Open Up!!!"

I immediately heard shouting and movement inside the house. Suddenly the back door opened and the suspect emerged holding a handgun.

I immediately yelled "Stop! FBI! Put the gun down!"

He looked at me and brought the gun up to aim at me. I developed what is known as tunnel vision and my only focus was on the gun in the suspect's hand. Before I knew it I had emptied the five blank shells from the shotgun and the six blank rounds from the revolver. When I went to reload, the suspect went back into the house.

It was training but those few moments felt incredibly real. My heart was pounding, my breath had quickened and my muscles tightened. Luckily, in my career I never had to fire a weapon in a real-life situation, but that training incident taught me how powerful the will to live can be.

It's the same phenomenon that occurs when police officers have to engage armed suspects and it's later reported the police fired excessively. What happens is a primal reaction that drives a person to stop the threat they see before them. I'm certain that critics in the wake of police shootings, who make allegations of overkill and speculate on what the officer should or should not have done, have never had a gun pointed or fired at them.

One thing I would like to add before I move on from my training at the FBI Academy. In my grandfather's day, the overall training was not very different except that new Special Agents were required at almost all times to wear a suit, tie and fedora. By the time I went through the training however, we were not required to wear a coat and tie but a uniform that consisted of a powder blue polo shirt, khaki slacks, a brown leather belt and black tennis shoes.

For anyone who saw the film "The Silence of the Lambs," the uniform worn by Jodie Foster at the start of the movie, which was filmed at the FBI Academy about six months before I got there, was the exact uniform my class wore. Several of the instructors from the Academy were in the film. And I can tell you that the scenes of Foster's character, Clarice Starling, going through the training, were very accurate.

The later scenes, where she is tracking down a serial killer, are strictly Hollywood. No actual field work would be done by a New Agent Trainee still in the Academy. Even after graduating and being given their first assignments, new FBI Agents are closely guided by veteran Agents and given very little leeway in what they do. But it was still a good movie.

After successfully completing the New Agent Training, I was sent to the Little Rock, Arkansas Field Office for my first assignment. I reported for duty in late September 1990. Little Rock was similar to East Texas in both culture and climate.

I was assigned primarily to bank fraud investigations. The work was not much different than I had been doing as an analyst in the Dallas office, the difference being I was now the one conducting the interviews, testifying in grand jury and, if necessary, at trial.

Little Rock was a small office with less than 50 Special Agents covering the whole state which meant in addition to my bank fraud investigations, I participated in all types of cases including bank robberies, kidnappings, and fugitive investigations.

In 1992, Bill Clinton was elected President and he appointed numerous people from Arkansas to White House positions. That required intensive background investigations. Being assigned a background investigation is not something Agents really enjoy doing, and so as a new Agent with almost no say in what cases were assigned to me, guess who got assigned the brunt of background investigations of White House appointees?

The Arkansas background investigations were routine and involved contacting references, employers and neighbors of the White House appointees. Two of the individuals that I did background work on were Webster Hubbell and Vince Foster.

Both were appointed to high level positions: Hubbell at the Justice Department and Foster at the White House. Everyone that I talked to praised them and had nothing bad to say at all. It was as if they had walked on water their whole lives.

However, after going to Washington, Foster committed suicide in 1993 and Hubbell pleaded guilty to wire fraud in 1994. I didn't participate in the investigations relating to Foster's suicide or Hubbell's criminal activities — but

I often wondered if maybe an Agent with more experience might have seen something in their backgrounds that I missed.

—

In 1995, I was transferred to the Chicago Field Office. As I mentioned earlier, the famous cases the FBI worked against the 1930s gangsters have fascinated me since I was a young boy. So to be in the city where a lot of those cases happened was tremendously exciting.

I went to a movie at the Biograph Theater, which was still in operation and had not changed much since Dillinger was killed there in 1934.

I was assigned to a squad in downtown Chicago investigating bankruptcy and government fraud. The cases were interesting and numerous — I know it's hard to believe there is government fraud in Chicago.

Since I lived out in the suburbs I commuted into downtown every day. At times the commute could take over two hours to go about 30 miles.

An opportunity opened up on the Special Operations Group (SOG), a full-time surveillance squad based out of an office not far my home in the suburbs. I didn't particularly want to do full-time surveillance, but I would no longer have those long daily commutes. Ironically enough however, I would spend way more time in the car.

Once I started with SOG, I fell in love with surveillance. Conducting surveillance is a little like fishing — you wait for that bite on your line, and when it happens it's very exciting. Surveillance is an essential law enforcement tool simply meant to observe subject's comings and goings to see who they meet with and where they go.

It is entirely carried out in unmarked vehicles, but can require at times following someone on foot. In a huge city like Chicago and its suburbs, a moving vehicle surveillance required very aggressive driving for all but the immediate car trailing the subject. The sheer amount of traffic meant if the surveillance team didn't stay relatively close to (but out of sight of) the subject vehicle, you could be left behind and not able to catch up and replace the trailing vehicle when needed.

Each vehicle in the surveillance team takes turns following the subject vehicle so they don't see the same car behind them for an extended period of time. We regularly followed Outfit (Chicago's version of the Mafia) guys and had involvement in all types of cases ranging from white collar crime to extortion and kidnapping. We worked days, nights, weekends and holidays.

Surveillance is an investigative technique that is done on the subject's schedule and most of them don't work nine to five. The work can be boring at times but potentially very dangerous.

The closest I ever came to getting in a gunfight occurred during a case I worked on as part of SOG. A Mexican drug gang kidnapped an innocent relative of a person in a competing gang.

The kidnappers demanded a large ransom payment to be placed near a car wash on the south side of Chicago. The victim's family contacted the FBI and SOG was assigned to conduct surveillance of the car wash. A member of the victim's family placed a backpack with the ransom money in it inside a trashcan at the car wash. Within a few minutes, two young Hispanic males approached the trashcan and one of them picked up the backpack and they immediately started walking away. They walked to a nearby bus stop and got on a Chicago bus. We began following the bus. As we were trailing the bus, one member of the surveillance team called out over our radio system that it appeared there was a counter surveillance team from the Mexican gang also following the bus.

As I mentioned earlier, a moving surveillance in a city with a lot of traffic can make keeping up with the subject (in this case the bus) very difficult without excessive speeding or maneuvers that could make it obvious to the subject they are being followed.

At one point the bus stopped at a red light. I was the lead surveillance vehicle and I stopped in an adjacent lane with one car in front of me. The additional members of the surveillance team were caught in some traffic behind and were furiously trying to catch up. So I was alone at the moment.

When the light turned green, the bus drove on but the car in front of me remained stopped. There were two males in the car and I quickly assumed they were part of the counter surveillance team trying to hinder me. They probably assumed I was law enforcement but they couldn't be sure so I did what I would have done in a normal circumstance: I honked the horn. But the car didn't move. The bus was getting away from me and I couldn't change lanes because of the traffic.

After a few more seconds the car in front of me slowly started forward through the intersection. Shortly after the car started moving, I saw the passenger turn around in his seat to face me and he was holding a long gun of some type – either a shotgun or rifle. It definitely appeared to me he was preparing to shoot. I had a shotgun with me and called out over the radio that I was behind a car that I believed had an armed subject. I developed that same tunnel vision and adrenaline rush I described earlier that occurred during a training session — only this time the bullets wouldn't be blanks.

As I was focused on the passenger with the long gun, I heard one of my team members call out over the radio that he had caught up and was a couple of cars behind me. Since our job was to follow the bus, I immediately turned onto a side street to avoid the situation of being outnumbered and possibly outgunned by the counter surveillance team. My team member stayed with the bus. The car with the armed subject continued forward.

By the time I circled back off the side street and joined up with several of my team members, the car had sped off. We put out a description of the car for Chicago PD to be on the alert but it wasn't seen again. The subjects on the bus were subsequently arrested when they got off the bus in a residential area. They were from Mexico and were initially reluctant to cooperate — they had more fear of the gang than being in trouble with the law. Subsequent investigation led to the successful return of the victim but the armed individuals in the car I was behind were never identified.

—

In September 1997, I was offered a voluntary transfer known in the FBI as an OP transfer to the Tyler, Texas Resident Agency, a satellite office administratively under the authority of the Dallas Field Office. OP stands for Office of Preference and these transfers are based on seniority. They are meant to alternately balance the experience of Agents assigned in a particular office and give a senior Agent a chance for an assignment of their choosing.

Any Special Agent in the FBI is subject to transfer "at the needs of the Bureau" but once an Agent receives an OP transfer, there is an unwritten rule that they will not be transferred again.

I was happy to get the transfer, because Tyler is my hometown and a great place to live. Although I enjoyed my time in Chicago, one thing I knew I would not miss was the cold weather and having to shovel snow during the winter. Believe it or not, shoveling show is a very physically demanding endeavor. It can be minus 10 degrees outside and you will actually break a sweat doing the work. But if you don't clear your driveway and sidewalk, that pretty snow will turn into a sheet of ice that will be there for days or weeks.

So when the movers were packing up the things in my garage, I told them they could leave the snow shovel for the folks moving in because I would never need one again in my life. Although we may get some snow or ice during winter in Texas, you can count on it being above 50 degrees in a day or two. So in early December 1997, I headed home for the Lone Star State.

—

In the large offices of the FBI like New York, Los Angeles and Chicago, Agents are assigned to separate squads investigating cases that address specific violations such as bank robbery, white collar crime, cybercrime, and more recently, terrorism.

In a Resident Agency (RA) however, individual Agents work all types of cases. As we say in the RA, "we work whatever comes in the door." Also, in a lot of RAs — and Tyler is no different — there is a fairly large territory comprised of several counties. Although Tyler has a population of about 100,000, most of the territory for the RA is rural, and small hamlets like Tenaha are very common.

The FBI is both a law enforcement and an intelligence agency. Since September 11, 2001, combating terrorism has been the overall top priority and is overseen by the intelligence side. On the law enforcement side, public corruption is the top priority.

Public corruption occurs when elected or appointed federal, state or local officials use the power of their offices or positions for some type of personal gain.

The illicit activity can take several forms and can occur in the executive, legislative and judicial branches of government at all levels. The majority of corruption cases I've worked have been of law enforcement officers. Unfortunately, this is probably a third of all public corruption cases addressed by the FBI.

In East Texas, and indeed most of rural America, law enforcement corruption often occurs when law enforcement officers protect drug dealers from arrest and prosecution. This sad fact is borne out of the large demand for drugs, primarily methamphetamine, and low pay for cops in those rural areas.

By its very nature, corruption involves conspiracy and "under the table" transactions. Those involved in the conspiracy have a mutual interest in protecting each other.

Because of this mutual protection, public corruption investigations are among the most difficult types of criminal cases to solve. Getting inside the conspiracy is the most effective way of proving the existence of corruption. This can be done in a couple of ways — — undercover agents or cooperating conspirators. Having someone inside the conspiracy provides intelligence about the extent of the corruption and those involved. Most importantly however, it allows the use of secret recordings to capture incriminating and illegal activity. It is very difficult to deny receiving a bribe payment if the money is counted out in front of you and it's all on video.

So at the beginning of any corruption investigation, finding someone to cooperate is key. In many cases both the corruption case and the cooperating witness are identified at the same time. This occurs when someone gets arrested on unrelated charges and reveals the corruption to lessen their potential punishment from the unrelated charges.

For example, a drug dealer gets arrested in another state or county with a large amount of drugs and reveals he is being protected by a police officer.

From that point, the drug dealer can record incriminating telephone calls, send and receive text messages and make protection payments that can be video recorded.

As an example, in 2007 an individual contacted the Tyler FBI office and revealed a possible plot by a Constable who wanted to begin manufacturing methamphetamine. Randy Thompson, a Constable from Cherokee County, south of Tyler, found a bag of white powder while on patrol and believed it was pseudoephedrine, a precursor chemical of methamphetamine.

Thompson told the individual, who was a mild acquaintance; he wanted to "cook" the pseudoephedrine into meth and sell it for easy money. The cooperating witness said he knew people who could cook the meth and would sell it for them. Thompson agreed and gave the witness the bag of white powder. Subsequent laboratory analysis confirmed it was pseudoephedrine.

With the help of the cooperating witness, Thompson was caught on videotape three separate times receiving cash payments for what he believed were profits from the illegal sale of methamphetamine. In recorded conversations between Thompson and the cooperating witness, Thompson was so pleased with the scheme that he was eager to continue. He talked about going to Mexico to buy large amounts of pseudoephedrine and the necessity of avoiding border authorities.

To avoid being caught on the border, Thompson said he would "recon their asses" and kill them if necessary. Thompson said "I would hate to have to kill anybody, but as an officer, I would be in a lot of trouble if I got caught."

After he was indicted on drug trafficking charges, we arrested Thompson at a state prison facility where he was employed as a Corrections Officer (he apparently only worked as a Constable, an elected position, part-time). Instead of being the tough guy he had been in the recorded conversations, Thompson meekly complied and admitted to the scheme. He received a 10-year federal prison sentence after pleading guilty. The case was relatively easy because of the cooperating witness. It likely would have gone undetected otherwise.

The point of the example is that without someone cooperating, it is very difficult to get enough compelling evidence to prove a corruption case. You will see this play out in the Tenaha investigation.

Civil rights cases are another high priority case in the FBI. The term "civil rights" is broadly defined as freedom from unequal treatment based on certain protected characteristics.

There can be both criminal and civil violations of civil rights. The FBI primarily pursues criminal civil rights violations and rarely has involvement in civil cases involving civil rights.

The specific types of criminal civil rights cases having the highest priority involve the use of threat or force by law enforcement officers against individuals in custody. Although I didn't see as many civil rights cases as public corruption cases, I worked my share of them.

One of them involved the in-custody beating of a county jail inmate by a Sheriff's Chief Deputy and CID (Criminal Investigative Division) Lieutenant. The inmate, who had the street name Chicken Hawk, was a long time criminal who had been arrested on drug charges. He was brought to the Chief Deputy's office to be interviewed. Chicken Hawk, who was handcuffed with his hands behind him, was placed in chair as the questioning began. Chicken Hawk acknowledged to me he was extremely belligerent and made threatening comments about the Lieutenant's son.

The Lieutenant became angry and punched Chicken Hawk hard enough to knock him out of the chair and onto the floor. The Chief Deputy then jumped on top of him and beat him further. After the beating, Chicken Hawk was escorted to jail and booked in. His bruised face in the book-in photo was great evidence.

There was a time when the beating of arrestees, especially arrestees who resisted, was routine and expected. But the times have changed, and such behavior by law enforcement officers is simply no longer tolerated.

Chicken Hawk, who was old enough to remember the old practices, told me "I probably deserved a beating and I'm only cooperating with you because they should have let me go instead of taking me to jail after they beat me up."

Some of the most famous cases of the FBI involved public corruption and civil rights investigations.

In 1978, the ABSCAM case (a codename based on a fictitious company named Abdul Enterprises) was a public corruption investigation that used undercover agents and concealed recordings to obtain the convictions of seven members of Congress on bribery charges related to the exchange of money for various political favors.

Operation Greylord in Chicago in the 1980s focused on judicial corruption and used undercover agents and cooperating witnesses to obtain over 90 convictions of crooked judges, lawyers, policemen and other officials. Its codename came from the wigs worn by British judges.

Two important civil rights investigations occurred in the 1960s: The 1963 bombing of the 16th Street Baptist Church in Birmingham, Alabama and the 1964 Mississippi Burning case in Philadelphia, Mississippi where three civil rights workers were killed by local members of the Ku Klux Klan.

Because of the political and racial realities of the Deep South in the 1960s, many white individuals suspected of killing African-Americans faced little threat of prosecution or conviction in friendly state courts. Except in the case of the President and other exceptions, murder is not a federal crime, and cases like the 16th Street bombing and Mississippi Burning were pursued federally as civil rights prosecutions to bring some measure of justice.

These investigations ultimately helped result in convictions in state court of the subjects involved, although for one subject in each case, justice came many years later. The investigations remained open, if inactive, in the hope that new evidence or witnesses could be located. In the Mississippi Burning case, Klansman Edgar Ray Killen was convicted of the murder of the three civil rights workers in 2005. In the 16th Street Baptist Church case, another Klansman, Bobby Frank Cherry, was convicted of murder in 2002.

I was part of the 16th Street Baptist Church bombing investigation long after it originally occurred in 1963. My part was small but important and had a unique coincidental detail. In the spring of 2000, I was assigned a "lead" to arrest Bobby Frank Cherry on a state arrest warrant issued in Alabama.

Cherry was retired and living in East Texas. He had long been suspected of involvement in the bombing that caused the deaths of four young African-American girls. I didn't do any investigative work on the case other than locate and arrest Cherry.

He was cooperative when he came to the door and I told him "Mr. Cherry you are under arrest on a warrant from Alabama for the 16th Street Baptist Church bombing."

He simply said "Oh."

I asked him if he had any weapons on him. Cherry said "just a .22 I keep in my pocket."

After retrieving the .22 pistol, and putting him in handcuffs, Cherry seemed resigned to the fact that his past had caught up with him. He was subsequently transferred back to Alabama where he was convicted at trial and later died in prison.

The coincidental detail of this arrest was the 16th Street Baptist Church bombing occurred on the exact day I was born. I didn't mention this to Cherry when I arrested him but I suspect the irony would not have been lost on him.

This case is a good example of how seriously these types of cases are taken by the FBI, and the tenacity with which they are worked — no matter how long it takes.

—

In 2009, when the initial allegations of the Tenaha case were reviewed, they appeared to involve violations of the Hobbs Act. The Hobbs Act specifically prohibits public officials, acting under color of law, from demanding or extorting money or other property from individuals. In the FBI, Hobbs Act investigations involving public officials are usually administratively documented as Public Corruption matters rather than Civil Rights cases. Because an investigation is opened administratively as a Public Corruption matter however, does not mean other violations will not be addressed and documented within the same case file. This fact will have importance later in this story.

The FBI opened the Tenaha investigation as a Public Corruption investigation because of the potential of Hobbs Act violations. Normally, when the FBI conducts an investigation, the results are presented to the United States Attorney's Office within a particular judicial district for prosecution. The U.S. Attorney reviews the witness interviews and evidence obtained and ultimately presents the case to a grand jury for an indictment. Should a matter go to trial, the U.S. Attorney's Office prosecutes the case in Federal District Court.

In certain cases however, including Civil Rights matters, the Department of Justice will often conduct the prosecution.

As the case in Tenaha had national attention — due to the CNN report — and because of the egregious nature of the allegations against law enforcement officers, including a District Attorney, the Department of Justice assigned a lawyer from their Civil Rights Section.

It is important to point out that some of the allegations contained in the 2008 *Morrow* civil lawsuit to which I have referred were in large part the basis for the initiation of the criminal case in Tenaha. Although parties to the civil lawsuit can provide information to criminal investigators and prosecutors, generally, information derived in the criminal case is not shared with parties to a civil case.

Also, for the clarification of the reader, a civil case, such as *Morrow*, is a legal dispute in which a plaintiff seeks relief — usually in the form of money — to compensate for damages. The plaintiff has the burden of proving their case by a preponderance of the evidence, meaning the court decides it is more likely than not the defendant is responsible.

In criminal cases however, the standard of proof is beyond a reasonable doubt, a much higher standard. The high standard exists because the result of a conviction in criminal court means an individual may lose their freedom and be sentenced to prison.

Finally, although the county in which Tenaha is located, Shelby County, is normally covered by the FBI through our Lufkin, Texas RA, I was assigned the case because I was not acquainted with any of the officers involved or the District Attorney and had no working relationship with anyone there.

The Texas Rangers assigned a Ranger who also had no previous relationships in Shelby County. This was done to ensure objectivity and integrity — something that would later be questioned by a surprising source.

And so began my odyssey in Tenaha, Texas.

2

THERE'S DRUGS AND MONEY
ON HIGHWAY 59

In November 2006, Barry Washington was hired as the Deputy City Marshal for Tenaha, Texas by Mayor George Bowers. This was an unusual situation because Washington was to be under the supervision of Mayor Bowers — and not City Marshal Fred Walker. In addition, Washington was to be paid a larger salary than Walker and had the opportunity for bonuses. I'm sure this wasn't a favorable situation for Walker, but as the Mayor was also his boss, there was nothing he could do.

To understand why Bowers hired Washington under such unique circumstances, it is important to know what Washington was known for. Barry Washington was legendary in law enforcement at narcotics interdiction. He had a lengthy career with the Texas Department of Public Safety (DPS) and had retired a couple of years earlier. He found life outside law enforcement unfulfilling and gladly accepted Mayor Bowers' offer to come to work in Tenaha.

Washington was well regarded by most everyone in law enforcement and had an exemplary record at DPS.

I learned from conversations with several Assistant United States Attorneys that Washington had testified numerous times in federal court on narcotics cases. He had even received official recognition for his efforts from the United States Attorney's Office.

Washington was also somewhat polarizing — I found that people either loved or hated him. He had an uncanny talent, though, for finding hidden compartments in cars and trailers where money or drugs were stashed.

Washington was also unique in that he spoke with a deep East Texas drawl, dressed like a cowboy, and was African-American. He had an easy-going manner that belied his reputation as a top-notch interdictor.

For readers unfamiliar with narcotics interdiction, it is a strategy used by law enforcement officers conducting routine car stops to catch individuals engaged in smuggling or transporting illegal drugs — or the massive amounts of money used to purchase drugs.

Once a car is stopped, an officer will engage the driver and passengers in simple conversation. While the conversation is ongoing, the officer will look for several indicators of possible drug trafficking — including strong odors from deodorizers, pro law enforcement stickers, the use of rental cars, multiple cell phones, religious artifacts or stickers, nervous behaviors and conflicting stories.

All these factors and more are assessed by the officer. If there is sufficient indication of suspicious activity, the officer will seek consent to search the vehicle. The driver does not have to consent to the search. In some cases however, the evidence of suspicious activity is strong enough — in other words, probable cause exists — that the officer doesn't need consent and can legally search the vehicle.

One key to successful interdiction is that the officer must assess all the suspicious indicators only within the time it reasonably takes to administer the traffic violation — that is, check driver's licenses and vehicle registrations, write up warning or actual citations. If a driver consents to having the vehicle searched, the second key to interdiction is spotting possible hidden compartments, because drug traffickers can be very creative in hiding their contraband. Barry Washington was expert at both and was considered to be one of the best at narcotics interdiction in the country.

Interdiction can be very successful, but it is also controversial. Allegations of racial profiling have been leveled because a large number of cases involve minorities. This, in part, became the basis of the 2008 *Morrow vs. City of Tenaha* federal civil case filed against Washington, District Attorney Lynda K. Russell, Mayor George Bowers, Constable Randy Whatley, and DA Investigator Danny Green, and the later criminal investigation to which I was assigned.

About two weeks after he was hired, Barry Washington conducted a car stop which led to the seizure of over $600,000 in cash hidden in Christmas packages in a car bound for Houston, Texas.

This brings us to another reason Mayor Bowers hired Barry Washington.

U.S. Route 59 is the main road through Tenaha. It runs from the United States border with Mexico at Laredo, Texas to the Canadian border in Minnesota. It crosses several interstates and is considered one of the top drug trafficking corridors in the country. Barry Washington largely earned his reputation in narcotics interdiction at the DPS working a stretch of U.S. 59 north of Tenaha near Carthage, Texas in Panola County.

After coming to Tenaha, Washington teamed up his interdiction efforts with Randy Whatley, the Shelby County Precinct 4 Constable. Whatley's office was based in Tenaha, not far from Washington's office at the City Marshal's Office. It made good sense for them to work together. Whatley had a narcotics detection dog, an asset that could come in handy as an additional tool in determining probable cause for a vehicle search. Also, Whatley had far less experience than Washington in conducting interdiction stops. So to a certain degree, Washington acted as a mentor for Whatley.

In Texas, a Constable is an elected position, primarily responsible for serving civil papers and acting as bailiffs for Justice of the Peace courts. However, a Constable is also a certified peace officer with full authority to enforce all state laws. This meant Whatley was fully authorized to conduct the interdiction stops with Washington.

Washington and Whatley worked out an agreement to alternate the duties of compiling and submitting investigative reports for each car stop they conducted that resulted in the seizure of drugs or money. Drugs were stored within evidence rooms located in their respective offices. When money was seized, District Attorney Lynda K. Russell or her investigator Danny Green would take possession of the money and deposit it into a bank account for forfeited funds.

The seized money, after it was officially forfeited through a court proceeding, would be split among the City Marshal's Office, the Constable's Office and the District Attorney's Office.

In Texas, money seized in drug trafficking or organized criminal activity can be used by city and county governments for law enforcement purposes only. However, there is wide discretion as to what constitutes an official law enforcement purpose. Seized money could be used to fund the purchase of police equipment or to hire more officers, for example — a clear law enforcement purpose.

However, whether or not it could be used for electioneering by the District Attorney, as would be found in this case, would be a question that at a minimum would raise suspicions, because it didn't look right — even if it was technically allowed.

With Barry Washington working interdiction on Highway 59 though, big time seizures of drugs would be a regular occurrence. But it also meant the city and county coffers of Mayor Bowers and DA Russell would start growing at a rapid pace.

3

I WOULD VOTE TO ACQUIT

By November 2010, I had been working the criminal case based off the Morrow civil allegations in Tenaha for 19 months. I had participated in numerous interviews, reviewed hundreds of documents, looked at hours of videotape of car stops, and testified in grand jury.

In looking at the cases of the individuals who had brought the civil lawsuit against the Tenaha officials and several other cases involving persons who had money seized on interdiction stops conducted by Barry Washington and Randy Whatley, two patterns emerged.

All the supposed victims involved had prior arrests involving narcotics and other criminal activity. Some had even been arrested on drug trafficking charges in other jurisdictions since they had been stopped in Tenaha.

The other pattern was the traffic violations allegedly committed by the victims, the reason they were stopped, appeared to have a legal, if not a common sense, basis.

In several of the cases, individuals were stopped by Washington or Whatley for traveling two miles over the speed limit, failing to signal a lane change, or riding in the passing lane too long. Although these innocuous violations are ignored by most police officers, they were routinely enforced in Tenaha. Despite the lack of materiality, Washington and Whatley were absolutely within the law to pull cars over for the minor moving violations.

There was another issue in the case. All the supposed victims of the car stops were African-American, Hispanic, or otherwise dark-skinned. This led to the allegation of racial profiling. Since Barry Washington himself was African-American, this argument had less weight, but I suppose it is possible for someone to profile against their own race.

It is not the purpose of this book to re-litigate the 2008 *Morrow vs. City of Tenaha* civil lawsuit, which ultimately resulted in the City of Tenaha settling out of court, but I will add my observations of the issue for context.

I reviewed hundreds of videotapes of car stops conducted by Washington and Whatley. There were far fewer done by Whatley than Washington. Barry Washington was prolific at stopping cars. He went literally from one stop to the next. I realized a large part of his success in interdiction was attributable to the same formula used by a successful salesman.

His success was based on making a large number of stops, quickly determining if probable cause existed for a search or determining if getting consent to search would be fruitful. If not, he moved on to the next one. A large number of stops, especially on U.S. Route 59, should statistically result in finding at least some cars that were transporting illegal drugs or money to purchase drugs.

I know my observations are anecdotal, as I didn't see every car stop done by Washington while he was employed in Tenaha or during his DPS career. However in the car stop videos I reviewed, which encompassed more than just the *Morrow* stops, there was no discernible racial pattern observed of those being stopped.

Washington stopped African-Americans, Hispanics, whites, males, females, young, and old. Nor did there seem to be a pattern of the types of cars stopped either. In a relaxed manner, Washington would engage the drivers, tell them about why he stopped them, ask about their destinations, make small talk, and eventually seek their consent to search the vehicle.

Most of the drivers consented. Sometimes Washington conducted cursory searches and sometimes the searches were more thorough. When drivers did not consent, unless there was other probable cause, he politely thanked them and sent them on their way. He would sometimes issue citations, but most often let them go with a warning. Washington wasn't concerned about writing traffic tickets. He was looking for people transporting drugs or money.

Another of the allegations made by the victims who had their money seized was they had been threatened with either jail or having their children taken away if they did not agree to sign a waiver of ownership of their cash.

After Barry Washington began conducting interdiction stops in Tenaha, the number of seizures of drugs and money greatly increased. District Attorney Investigator Danny Green designed a form he began using at the car stops that allowed individuals to sign away their money with the promise they would not later contest the seizure and would face criminal charges if they did.

It was a common sense idea, meant to make the process easier. There were a couple of big problems, though.

The Texas Legislature outlawed the procedure years earlier, and because a judge was not involved, it was arguably a deprivation of a suspect's due process rights under the law.

The use of signed waivers to document the seizure of money, however, was done only for a short period of time and only a few individuals signed them. Washington denied ever using the forms or even hearing the term "waiver" used in the context of the car stops. This denial would cause us problems later on in the case.

One other part of the case that gave some credence to charges of corruption was the lack of prosecutions of the people involved in the car stops whose money had been seized.

If you assume the searches were done on the basis of probable cause, then the fact that few resulted in prosecutions is troubling. It gave the appearance the stops were made just for the money.

But the money seized by Washington and Whatley in their stops was taken pursuant to violations of either money laundering or organized criminal activity statutes under Texas law. This is appropriate, when a lawful search reveals the individuals to be in possession of large amounts of cash for which they cannot provide a reasonable explanation.

All of the investigative files related to the plaintiffs in *Morrow vs. City of Tenaha* and other stops not part of the lawsuit were reviewed extensively by the FBI and DOJ. In my opinion, the files were fairly thorough, especially by small town law enforcement standards, and would have been mostly sufficient for presentation to a state grand jury.

Either through incompetence or laziness, District Attorney Lynda K. Russell failed to pursue prosecutions against any of the plaintiffs of *Morrow*. Even more suspicious — several individuals later hired attorneys after their respective car stops and instead of being prosecuted, as the waiver agreement stated, Russell returned their money without a hearing. This furthered the impression it was just about money.

Although there were a few purchases made by the DA with seized funds that stretched whether there was a law enforcement purpose, there was no clear indication DA Russell, or any other of the officers were personally profiting from the stops.

Much was made in the "Anderson Cooper 360" CNN segment about a $10,000 check to Barry Washington from the City of Tenaha. Although I don't personally agree with the policy, it was an agreement Washington had when he was hired as a Deputy City Marshal that he would get bonuses for his performance. Again, it was something that was technically legal but on the surface, it smacked of impropriety.

Despite these aspects of the case — which admittedly looked bad — nothing, in my opinion, was found that clearly indicated violations of federal law. Remember, the standard of proof for conviction in a criminal case is beyond a reasonable doubt.

Although Washington and Whatley had engaged in very aggressive interdiction techniques, Investigator Danny Green had implemented a questionable use of a waiver form, and DA Russell's lack of prosecutions in lieu of seizing money, nothing in my opinion proved criminal violations had occurred in relation to the car stops — beyond a reasonable doubt.

Had I been sitting on jury I would have voted to acquit. Not because I didn't think some violations might have occurred, but it's my opinion we couldn't prove them with what we had, after conducting an extensive investigation.

But my opinions, I would find, didn't mean much to my own prosecutor.

4

THE DOJ

The case, at this point, reached something of a stalemate between the FBI and the Department of Justice (DOJ).

The stalemate was caused largely by disagreements over what the evidence gathered to date actually proved. Jeff Millslagle, a veteran agent who was working with me on the case, and our supervisor, John Jones, both agreed with me that we had very little in the way of convicting anyone in criminal court.

Lead Department of Justice Attorney Myesha Braden, however, was unconvinced. Braden, who was based out of Washington, D.C., had a theory regarding the relationship between prosecutor and investigator that was new to me.

Traditionally the investigator does the leg work on an investigation. This includes conducting victim and witness interviews; identifying, obtaining, and reviewing relevant documents and records; collecting and maintaining evidence; and ultimately testifying in grand jury and trial. This is the heart and soul of what an investigator does.

The prosecutor is consulted and briefed throughout the investigation. The prosecutor certainly gives input and direction for an investigation, but rarely is involved in the day-to-day execution.

When a case is presented to a Grand Jury, the investigator testifies to the facts of the case. If an indictment is obtained, this is when the heavy lifting begins for the prosecutor. The prosecutor begins to fine-tune the case and may conduct victim and witness interviews in preparation for trial. At this point, the investigator's role is to support trial preparation — which is entirely dictated by the prosecutor.

Braden's theory worked a lot differently. She acted as both investigator and prosecutor. She directed who was to be interviewed, gave express orders that no interviews should be done without her being present or without her consent, and she took the lead on all interviews.

I came to realize Braden only wanted investigators at the interviews to take notes and write up reports. I believe if she had been able to act as her own witness and directly present facts, rather than through an independent witness, she would have sought no involvement of the FBI.

At one point, her disdain for the FBI was apparent when she told Jones, Millslagle and I that without her, we were "just guys with badges asking questions."

Indeed, along the way she removed both the Texas Attorney General's Office and the Texas Rangers from their roles assisting in the case.

Early on in the investigation, I coordinated with the Texas AG and the Texas Rangers. Both agencies had received complaints about Tenaha and they were under a little bit of political pressure to address the issue.

I had two or three telephone conversations with attorneys from the AG's office. I passed along Braden's name to them for additional coordination. Braden had a subsequent meeting at the AG's office, to which I was not invited. I don't know the substance of the meeting but I was informed afterwards by Braden that the Texas AG's office would no longer be involved in the case.

I also coordinated with the Texas Rangers at the outset of the case. Many times, state and federal violations overlap and by joining together, each agency can bring their unique resources to the investigation. In a matter as complicated as the Tenaha case, I was happy to have help from the Texas Rangers. They assigned Ranger Steve Jeter. I had never worked with Jeter before, but after our first meeting, he impressed me as a solid and objective investigator.

Jeter and I conducted some initial interviews at the Shelby County Sheriff's Office. It was after these brief interviews that I learned from Braden that she not only wanted to be involved in the interviews, but she was also going to dictate who was interviewed. Because she was based out of Washington D.C., interviews had be set up in advance to fit her schedule.

One of the interviews set up for Braden was that of Shelby County DA Investigator Danny Green. Green was potentially a powerful witness. Although he had not performed any of the car stops, he responded on many of them, especially stops involving money. This process was followed because of Washington's personal policy of handing over seized money immediately to the District Attorney's Office.

As I pointed out earlier, in cases involving corruption, it is vital to have a cooperating witness inside the conspiracy. Green would have been perfect because he was in a position to give testimony about the conduct of Barry Washington, Constable Randy Whatley and District Attorney Lynda K. Russell, who was alleged to be using the seized funds for personal use.

But any chance Green would be a cooperating witness was lost after Braden's interview of him. Because of a prior commitment, I was unable to participate in Greens' interview. Ranger Jeter agreed to help out with the interview and sit in with Braden. In setting up the interview, Jeter could only get Green to agree to it if it was conducted in a public place.

They agreed on meeting at the Dairy Queen in Center, Texas. This may sound unusual to the reader, but many times reluctant witnesses are more comfortable meeting with investigators in public places. I have met witnesses many times in strange places of their choosing, including a Dairy Queen, to gain cooperation I might not otherwise get.

Braden was appalled at the idea of meeting with Green in a Dairy Queen. She made no secret of her displeasure about it. Prior to the interview, Braden told Ranger Jeter she would be asking the interview questions because she did not trust Jeter to be objective against another law enforcement officer. Jeter was greatly offended, as he should have been, but in the interest of cooperation and professionalism, he went ahead and participated in Green's interview.

I knew the Green interview must not have gone well when Jeter called me and said "What in the world have you gotten me involved in?"

In addition to Braden questioning his objectivity, he said she angered Green during the interview — making his cooperation unlikely. Shortly after the Green interview, Braden ordered me to cease cooperation with the Texas Rangers. I reluctantly did so, only because FBI executive management in Dallas did not want a fight with the Department of Justice on such a sensitive case.

Beyond our differences about the roles of prosecutor and investigator, Braden and I disagreed on the merits of the criminal case we were working. Millslagle and I both believed the evidence obtained and the interviews conducted up to that point failed to reveal criminal violations by the law enforcement officers involved.

Millslagle had been in the FBI longer than me and I greatly respected his opinion when he said "I just don't see a case here."

Braden felt we lacked objectivity and were protecting the officers out of some misplaced loyalty to law enforcement. I assured her our only loyalty was to the truth, and told her about the case I successfully worked against the officers who went to prison for severely beating the inmate street named Chicken Hawk. I was mildly acquainted with one of the officers prior to the beating and had played golf with him in a charity tournament — but I did not let that affect my objectivity when I worked the case. The story had absolutely no impact on her outlook toward us.

Braden seemed convinced we were attempting to somehow sabotage the case. Any input that was contrary to her vision of the case was met with scorn and derision. In the course of a long career with the FBI, I had never had my objectivity questioned, especially by someone who was supposed to be on my side — who I simply disagreed with over the interpretation of findings.

Because of our different opinions and a deteriorating working relationship with Braden, I asked to have the case re-assigned to another agent. It was subsequently re-assigned to a veteran agent who also had difficulty dealing with Braden.

Ultimately, no criminal charges resulted from the DOJ investigation against any of the Tenaha or Shelby County officials. The best Braden was able to do — ironically, through intimidation tactics similar to those that were described by the Tenaha victims in *Morrow* — was get Constable Randy Whatley and DA Investigator Danny Green to give up their Texas peace officers licenses, under threat of prosecution.

Barry Washington, given the same offer, steadfastly refused, claiming he had done nothing wrong and would fight if prosecuted. He effectively called the DOJ's bluff and it worked. No prosecutive action was ever taken against him by the DOJ.

You might think my involvement in Tenaha would have come to an end at that point. But that changed a few days later, when I opened an envelope sent to me by Tenaha City Marshal Fred Walker.

5

JACK FROST

Fred Walker had served with several law enforcement agencies throughout his career, including the Texas Department of Public Safety, the Shelby County Sheriff's Office, and the San Augustine, Texas and Timpson, Texas Police Departments.

He had been interviewed several times in the course of the DOJ Civil Rights investigation. Although he had participated in a support role in several of the car stops conducted by Barry Washington and Randy Whatley, he had not been named as a defendant in *Morrow vs. City of Tenaha, et al.*

My opinion of Walker was positive, based the previous interviews — although his information overall was only marginally helpful to the investigation. My opinion would change in the months ahead.

In November 2010, Walker mailed me two separate but identical letters, one of which had a key taped to it. Although Walker had called me several times previously on other matters, I was not aware the letters were being sent to me until I opened them. Walker and an individual named Roderrete McClure each received a letter at their respective mailing addresses.

The letters were each two pages and were from someone calling himself Jack Frost. Frost claimed to be a DEA Agent. He demanded $70,000 each from Walker and McClure for the opportunity to buy their way out of trouble.

Frost claimed he was aware Walker and McClure had an organization that was making millions selling seized drugs from an evidence locker and Frost wanted part of it. It was clearly an extortion demand.

Frost instructed Walker and McClure to put the money, in large bills, in Post Office Box 332 at a UPS Store in Round Rock, Texas near Austin, within three days. The key, which had been taped to one of the letters, was for the post office box. After placing the money in the post office box, Frost instructed them to notify him through an email address he provided. Frost gave the warning that he would "burn the both of you down" if they looked for him.

Although by the time I received the letters, the three-day deadline Jack Frost set had passed, I immediately called Fred Walker.

To backtrack for a moment, just a few days prior to my receipt of the extortion letters, Fred Walker campaigned for and had been elected as the Shelby County Precinct 4 Constable — the position that had been vacant since Randy Whatley resigned it in 2009. When Walker answered my call, I congratulated him on the new position. I didn't realize then that his election would be connected to Jack Frost until several months later.

I asked him "Who do you think would send this to you?"

"I don't have any idea who did it or why they would have done it," he said.

He had received no other letters nor had anyone tried to contact him.

"Who all has handled the letters?" I asked, so we would know for elimination purposes if subsequent fingerprint analysis was done.

He assured me there had been minimal handling of the letters.

"Who is Roderrete McClure was and why would he be getting one of the letters," I asked.

"He is a local computer repair shop owner who previously worked for the city water department," Walker said. "I don't know why he would get a letter, either."

The Jack Frost letter was intriguing. It was bold. Frost was attempting to extort money from a law enforcement officer who he claimed was involved in a drug trafficking organization. Despite working in Tenaha for the previous year and a half, I had heard nothing even hinting at Walker being involved with drugs.

While I pondered whether there was any truth to Frost's claims, I considered Walker and McClure to be either victims of an extortion plot or more likely a hoax. But because Frost was claiming to be a DEA Agent and had left a trail that would make identifying him fairly easy, I thought it would be worth pursuing.

Normally, any potential federal violations occurring in Tenaha or Shelby County would be investigated by the Lufkin, Texas Resident Agency. As I was no longer involved in the DOJ investigation of the Civil Rights violations alleged there, I referred the extortion letters to the Lufkin RA. Lufkin is an office with a smaller staff and each agent carries a large workload. And because the demand date in the extortion letter had passed, and Walker and McClure had received no further threats, the case was made a low priority.

In February of 2011, I passed through Tenaha on an unrelated investigation to interview a witness, so I stopped in to meet the new City Marshal, Tom Reader. Reader replaced Fred Walker after he was elected as a Shelby County Constable the previous November. Reader was the Tenaha City Marshal back in the 1990s and left to pursue other opportunities. Mayor George Bowers asked Reader to return when the position opened.

Reader said since taking over he observed that Fred Walker, now the Precinct 4 Constable based in Tenaha, was spending a great deal of time at the home of Rod McClure.

"Fred Walker spends several hours a day at Rod McClure's house," he told me.

This didn't make sense to Reader.

"McClure has a lengthy criminal history and the word on the street is he's dealing drugs," he said. "I've known Rod a long time. I arrested him back in 1995 for shooting and wounding his cousin over a dispute."

Although I was no longer involved in anything in Tenaha, hearing this piqued my interest.

"Fred Walker told me Rod McClure was just a computer technician," I said. "He didn't mention he had a long criminal history and was a reputed drug dealer."

Since the Jack Frost letter mentioned the theft of drugs from an evidence locker, it might be relevant to know of McClure's history and reputation. So why wouldn't Walker have at least mentioned it to me? The fact Walker and McClure spent so much time together was also curious.

I confirmed McClure's criminal history. It included arrests for Robbery, Larceny, Unlawfully Carrying a Weapon, Theft by Check, Theft of Property, Attempted Sexual Assault, Assault – Family Violence, Terroristic Threat, Reckless Driving, and Criminal Trespass. All of these occurred at various times throughout the 1990s and early 2000s.

Regarding the 1995 shooting of his cousin, Cecil Moss[1], in an altercation

---

[1] Throughout this book, the names of witnesses whose identities did not become public have been changed.

in Tenaha, Reader told me "McClure fled Tenaha and they arrested him in Longview. I had to go get him and bring him back to Shelby County."

He continued "I later got a call from the Tyler DEA office and the Agent told me McClure was an informant and they suspected him of dealing drugs."

Reader said charges against McClure were subsequently dropped at the request of the DEA, despite their suspicions regarding him. Reader added there were also rumors all over Tenaha that McClure burned his own home down in 2008 as an insurance scam.

Reader's information about McClure's background and McClure's close relationship with Fred Walker were interesting, especially when considered in the context of some burglaries that occurred in Tenaha in 2009 and 2010.

The burglaries were something that didn't normally fall under FBI jurisdiction so I didn't pay much attention to them when they occurred.

In August 2010, the Tenaha City Marshal's Office was burglarized and several hundred pounds of marijuana stolen from the evidence room. In 2009, there had been burglaries at the Constable's Office in Tenaha and a Tenaha federal firearms dealer's shop.

For a town of 1000 people, something was very suspicious about three prominent burglaries, two of which were law enforcement offices.

At the time, neither of those offices were manned 24 hours a day.

Because of my familiarity of Tenaha gained during the DOJ investigation, I requested the Jack Frost extortion case be re-assigned to me. It was possible that Frost's claims of knowing about an illegal narcotics organization using drugs from an evidence locker may have had substance.

The United States Attorney's Office assigned an experienced prosecutor to the case. Her name was Lisa Flournoy. I wrote up an informal summary of what I knew at that point and I forwarded it to her.

After that, I met Lisa in a meeting on an unrelated case, and we briefly talked about the Tenaha case.

"I read your write-up on the new case in Tenaha," she said. "It sure doesn't look like a routine case."

Neither Lisa Flournoy, whose main expertise was in drug-related cases, nor I could have imagined how far from routine the case would be. Also, unlike working with Department of Justice attorneys, Lisa followed the more traditional model and did not get overly involved in the day-to-day work of the investigation.

The next step was to begin working on identifying Jack Frost. Which wasn't hard to do at all.

The post office box Frost instructed Walker and McClure to deposit the extortion money, Box 332 at the UPS Store in Round Rock, Texas, had been rented to Darla Cabot[2] a few days before the Jack Frost letters had been sent on October 22, 2010. Cabot had provided a driver's license photo and proof of insurance.

The insurance card listed the Vehicle Identification Numbers (VIN) of two vehicles. Both VINs came back to cars registered to Terrence Ford[3] of McKinney, Texas. In addition, after obtaining insurance records, we found the proof of insurance card presented to the UPS Store had been altered to reflect Darla Cabot's name rather than Terrence Ford's name. The VINs on the card given to the UPS store had not been altered and were accurately assigned to Ford.

The email address Jack Frost provided in the extortion letter was created from an IP address that was traced to Ford's McKinney, Texas address and was also created a few days before the letters were sent.

I obtained Ford's telephone records and this is where the case changed.

—

I found hundreds of calls and texts between Ford and McClure. Also, there were several calls and texts between Ford and Walker, though far fewer. Perhaps Ford knew about an illegal narcotics operation and stolen drugs from an evidence locker because of his almost constant telephone contact with McClure, and Ford decided to extort him with that information. There were several such possibilities and I wasn't sure what the truth was.

Ford's phone records also linked him to Darla Cabot, the person who rented the post office box to be used in the extortion. Cabot's driver's license (which I had confirmed was valid) listed a Dallas address. I found no connection however with Cabot to McClure or Walker, nor was there any evidence she had lived in or near Tenaha.

Since my suspicion that the previous Tenaha burglaries may have had some relevance to the scheme outlined in the Jack Frost letter, I contacted Texas Ranger Tom Davis. Davis was a veteran Ranger who had covered Shelby

---

[2] Not her real name.

[3] Not his real name.

County for several years. He investigated the burglaries of both the Tenaha City Marshal's Office in 2010 and Shelby County Constable's Office in 2009. No arrests had been made in either case.

"I was suspicious that the burglary at the City Marshal's Office was staged almost from the minute I got there," Davis told me. "There was a door apparently staged to look like the entry door, because all the glass was knocked out of it but it still had old cobwebs intact between the door and the top casing."

This meant the door had not been opened and entry was gained another way. However, no other doors or windows were damaged.

Davis said when he first arrived at the burglary scene, he asked Walker "Did the surveillance cameras pick up anything?"

Walker told Davis "I took the hard drives to Rod McClure to see if he could extract the footage."

At the time, Davis was not familiar with McClure. However, District Attorney's Investigator Kevin Windham, who replaced former Investigator Danny Green, one of the defendants in the *Morrow* lawsuit, was familiar with McClure. He found it suspicious that Walker would have so quickly released evidence from a crime scene to a civilian with McClure's history.

Indeed, because Walker's agency was the victim of this crime, proper procedure would have been for an independent agency to conduct the investigation. Walker, who discovered the burglary, should have simply secured the office and allowed the Rangers and the District Attorney's Office to process it as a crime scene.

In another breach of procedure, Walker recovered a threatening letter, handwritten in Spanish, which he was very anxious to ensure Ranger Davis looked at.

The letter, roughly translated, said "We are the Zetas and are aware of Tenaha through the CNN segment and we are going to kill all the gringo cops there." The Los Zetas are a ruthless drug syndicate that originally began as the enforcement arm of the Gulf Cartel, one of the oldest organized crime groups in Mexico.

Walker also said he found a Mapquest map that was printed out at 7:02 p.m. on August 21, 2010, showing a route from Brownsville, Texas to Tenaha, a distance of 554 miles and a driving time of over 8 hours.

Davis was immediately suspicious of both the Zetas letter and the Mapquest printout.

"I doubt very seriously that a Mexican drug cartel would leave a note like that and they certainly wouldn't bring the map of their purported trip into the place they were burglarizing" he said.

He subsequently took all the printers from the Marshal's Office as evidence to determine if the Mapquest printout had been printed on one of them.

It seemed preposterous that a Mexican gang located in Brownsville would drive more than eight hours to burglarize a law enforcement office they were unaware wasn't manned 24 hours.

Also, Walker's timeline of events didn't quite fit. Walker told Ranger Davis and Investigator Windham he had been at the office until almost midnight. Walker said he discovered the burglary about 6:50 a.m. the next morning. So assuming the burglars printed out the map in Brownsville at 7:02 p.m., drove the eight and a half hours, they would have arrived in Tenaha at the earliest around 3:30 a.m.

This gave them a maximum window of three hours to conduct the burglary of the Marshal's Office. Considering there was extensive ransacking, several hundred pounds of marijuana and other seized narcotics painstakingly taken from individually sealed boxes, and time for surveillance of the office to ensure no one was there, that didn't leave much time for the burglary to happen. Not to mention the Marshal's Office was located in a former bank building, prominently located on U.S. Route 59, the main thoroughfare through Tenaha, making the risk of being seen or caught very high.

One other fact was noticed by Ranger Davis and Investigator Windham during their assessment of the crime scene: The evidence room which had stored several hundred pounds of seized marijuana was not ventilated and yet had no detectable odor of marijuana.

Windham later told me "With all that marijuana, you can't tell me it wouldn't have smelled to high Heaven in there."

Even though it had presumably been removed only a few hours earlier, the smell of that much marijuana would have still been present. This implied the marijuana had never been there, or had been removed much earlier.

Ranger Davis also told me about the September 2009 burglary of the Precinct 4 Shelby County Constable's Office, which is located in Tenaha about 500 yards from the City Marshal's Office.

"The burglars entered through a rear glass door after they broke out the glass," he said. "Then they pried open the locked door to the evidence room."

Unlike the Marshal's Office burglary, though, there was very little ransacking and there did not appear to be a great deal of evidence missing.

"We weren't able to find an inventory of the evidence items so it was difficult to know exactly what was missing," Davis said.

The Constable's Office had been unmanned for about three months because Constable Randy Whatley resigned from the elected position in June 2009.

There was a way to establish, circumstantially at least, what was missing from both burglaries: Empty boxes recovered from both crime scenes had labels permanently affixed to them from the Texas Department of Public Safety Laboratory.

As Ranger Davis explained to me, "the lab labels have unique numbers that are assigned to each piece of evidence — in this case it would be narcotics. The unique number can be traced back to the lab and they can tell us the exact type and amount of drugs that were sealed inside."

Coincidence or not, almost all the missing drugs, which consisted primarily of marijuana and prescription drugs, were seized by Barry Washington and Randy Whatley during the car stops previously investigated in the DOJ investigation.

Cases involving drug seizures had not been reviewed as thoroughly however as stops involving money. But just like the money seizure cases, District Attorney Lynda K. Russell had been slow or inactive in prosecuting the matters and so the seized drugs were left sitting in the Marshal's and Constable's Offices pending some type of prosecutorial action for months or years.

At this point in the investigation, it was not wise to exclude anyone as a suspect. But one thing that tended to exonerate Washington and Whatley of involvement was their consistent submission of seized drugs to the DPS Lab for analysis after each individual stop.

I learned from my review of the Tenaha investigative files that narcotics evidence was routinely submitted by both Washington and Whatley to the lab almost immediately after seizure.

I reasoned to Davis, "if they intended to sell the drugs, as described in the Jack Frost letter, it would have been stupid for them to create an official chain of custody by submitting the drugs to the lab of an independent law enforcement agency."

Also, Jack Frost hadn't mentioned Washington and Whatley in the extortion letter — only Fred Walker and Rod McClure.

Davis and I both agreed it was likely the Jack Frost letters and the burglaries were somehow linked. Over the course of the next couple of months, it was necessary to finish some analysis of additional telephone records and other background work before conducting interviews of Ford, Walker, and McClure.

Also, during this period of time the new Tenaha City Marshal Tom Reader told me about an individual named David Thompson who apparently committed suicide in January 2010.

"David Thompson was a known drug dealer and he was very close to Rod McClure," Reader told me. "He's supposed to have committed suicide after the Secret Service ran a search warrant at his house for child porn. And Fred Walker was the only person to investigate it."

At the time, I didn't find it particularly unreasonable for someone to commit suicide after being accused of or implicated in child pornography. I did wonder, however, if Thompson's friendship with McClure had any connection to the Jack Frost letters or the Marshal's Office burglary.

Also during this period of time in the early summer of 2011, Reader turned over to me a Dell laptop computer owned by the City Marshal's Office that was previously used by Fred Walker when he was City Marshal.

Walker stepped down as City Marshal when he was elected as Precinct 4 Constable in November 2010 and took with him a city owned laptop. After numerous requests from Reader following Walker's resignation for him to return the laptop, Walker finally returned it about two months later.

Reader had the laptop forensically analyzed. Hundreds of photographs were recovered, most of which were personal and of no evidentiary value. However, among the photographs were several of McClure and members of his family on a hunting trip.

There were a few photos in which McClure was seen to be shouldering a hunting rifle. Since he was a convicted felon, it was illegal under federal law for him to be in possession of a firearm. Again, this was nothing that was going to make or break the case, but it was curious that Walker, a known law enforcement officer, would have personal photographs of a convicted felon carrying a hunting rifle.

Because the Jack Frost extortion letter mentioned that Walker and McClure were making millions from their drug organization, I obtained bank records for both Walker and McClure for 2010. My analysis revealed both had made consistent cash deposits ranging in amounts from $1,000 to $3,000 over the course of the year.

In August 2010 alone, McClure made cash deposits totaling $11,000 into the Computer Clinic account and for the year totaled almost $83,000. Walker's cash deposits were not as much, but were over and above his regular salary as City Marshal. McClure's income from his computer repair business showed some deposits and there was a small steady paycheck from his wife but no clear explanation for what he was doing to make regular cash deposits. It wasn't the millions described by Jack Frost, but it definitely hinted McClure and Walker were making money from something that generated cash consistently.

The one final area of investigation prior to interviewing Walker, McClure, and Ford was analysis of the handwritten Spanish language letter recovered by Walker at the scene of the Tenaha City Marshal's Office burglary.

The letter, which stated the Los Zetas planned to kill "gringo" cops, and listed Barry Washington, Fred Walker, Randy Whatley, Mayor George Bowers, and DA Lynda K. Russell. The letter seemed absurd but because Walker had been so insistent in giving it to Ranger Tom Davis at the Marshal's Office burglary scene, I thought it deserved some attention.

One day in his office, Tom Reader asked me if there was any value to some personal items left at the Marshal's Office by Marilyn Andrews[4] , a volunteer who acted as Fred Walker's secretary.

"I've asked Fred Walker several times if Marilyn Andrews is going to come by and pick up these items," he said, indicating a datebook and some greeting cards. "It's been so long now I'm going to throw them away because I consider it abandoned property."

I glanced through the items and noted a potentially important clue: The datebook and the greeting cards contained handwriting that looked remarkably like the handwriting in the Zetas letter.

I photocopied several pages from the datebook and thereafter painstakingly compared individual letters contained in the Zetas letter and Andrews' writing from the datebook and greeting cards. Although I'm not a handwriting expert, numerous individual letters compared side by side were so similar in construction and style, I was convinced the Zetas letter had been written by Andrews.

Subsequently however, the investigation revealed I was dead wrong about the authorship of the letter. The actual author, whom we found later, would provide yet another wild and unexpected twist in this case.

Finally this brought the next phase of the case which was to interview Fred Walker, Rod McClure and Terrence Ford. The case was getting very interesting indeed — but we were only scratching the surface.

---

[4] Not her real name.

6

HOW DID WE STUMBLE INTO WIRETAPPING?

On the morning of Monday, August 8, 2011, a team consisting of four FBI Agents and two Texas Rangers set out to contact and interview Fred Walker, Rod McClure, and Terrence Ford. None of the interviews were set up prior and we did not contact anyone in law enforcement in Shelby County. We wanted to talk to each of them separately and simultaneously. This would ideally catch each of them unprepared and unable to prepare a common story.

Interview of Ford:

Two FBI Agents went to McKinney, Texas to the home of Terrence Ford, one FBI Agent and one Texas Ranger contacted Fred Walker, and Ranger Tom Davis and I contacted Rod McClure.

Ford, who was at home when the Agents arrived, initially was willing to talk but wanted to do so in the front yard because he said his home smelled of cat urine. One of the Agents later told me smelling cat urine might have been better than sweating profusely while standing in the sweltering August heat.

Ford initially said he didn't know anyone named Darla Cabot. He was then presented with the fact Cabot had opened the post office box mentioned in the Jack Frost extortion letter using an insurance card that had VIN numbers of cars registered to him.

Ford then said "Oh that, well that was just part of a joke."

"I've known Rod for several years but I haven't had any recent contact," he said.

As the interview continued in his front yard, Ford offered, "I'm probably going to jail because of those letters I sent to Rod and Fred asking them for money."

Ford reiterated he did it as a joke and added, "there's rumors all over Tenaha that Rod and Fred are selling drugs."

Ford admitted knowing Darla Cabot. He said Cabot was a friend of his who agreed to open the post office box to help him play the joke. Ford said he didn't tell Cabot who he was playing the joke on, and she didn't know Walker or McClure.

Ford acknowledged typing the Jack Frost letters on his home computer and setting up the email address referenced in the letter. Ford said after receiving the letter, McClure called him and was extremely upset.

Ford said "Rod told me that he forwarded the letter to the FBI. I got real scared and didn't tell him that I sent the letter and it was a big joke. I just hoped it would go away."

The interview concluded with Ford remaining emphatic he sent the Jack Frost letters as a joke. He said he was open to answering any further questions and wanted to resolve the matter. The agents gave him my name and number. It didn't take him long to call.

Interview of Walker:

Walker was contacted and agreed to come by the City Marshal's Office for an interview. He was immediately confronted with the suspicious findings related to the Marshal's Office burglary which gave the appearance the burglary was staged. Walker acknowledged the cobwebs still attached at the top of the supposed entry door looked very suspicious, but he could offer no explanation.

Asked why he turned over the surveillance camera hard drives to Rod McClure before the Texas Rangers or the District Attorney's Office arrived at the scene, Walker said he had done so at the request of Tenaha Mayor George Bowers[5].

Walker was asked if he was aware of McClure's criminal history and if he knew McClure was a convicted felon.

"I don't know that I've never checked his CCH," he said, using a term commonly used in law enforcement indicating a person's criminal history.

I found this completely lacking in credibility, as numerous people in Tenaha were aware of McClure's status as a registered sex offender stemming from an attempted sexual assault. Several witnesses had asserted Walker and

---

[5] This assertion was subsequently denied by Mayor Bowers.

McClure spent many hours together each day and I knew from telephone records they were in almost constant contact.

Walker was asked about the handwritten Spanish language letter he recovered at the scene of the Marshal's Office burglary. The letter-by-letter comparison I did of handwriting from the Zetas letter and Marilyn Andrews' handwriting was shown to Walker. He acknowledged the writing was indeed almost exactly the same but denied knowing anything about Andrews writing the letter.

Although I would later learn Walker knew who actually wrote the letter, his denial that Andrews had anything to do with it was truthful.

Regarding his investigation of the death of David Thompson, Walker said he recovered the .32 caliber pistol found with Thompson's body and took photographs of the scene. Although not specific he said he secured both in the City Marshal's Office.

When confronted that a simultaneous search of the Marshal's Office failed to find either the pistol or photographs, Walker simply said "I don't know where they would be."

—

It is important for you to understand as I describe the interviews of Ford, Walker, and McClure, that they were ongoing nearly simultaneously and the investigators were communicating either by telephone conversation or text messaging. This was done to compare what was being learned in each interview — as they happened — to assess the truthfulness of each person.

So I will briefly detail some claims made by McClure before I fully detail our interview with him, so the information can be assessed in the context of Walker's interview.

While Walker's interview was ongoing, McClure, who was being interviewed by Davis and I, alleged that Walker had requested and authorized him to plant electronic recording devices in the offices of Barry Washington at the Tenaha City Marshal's Office and the Tenaha City Hall offices of Mayor George Bowers.

Davis texted this information back to FBI Agent Terry Lane, who was conducting the interview of Walker.

Walker initially claimed he did not recall anything about electronic bugging taking place at either the City Marshal's Office or at City Hall. However, after Velcro strips which McClure stated were used to hide the recording devices were found under the desk of Barry Washington — exactly where McClure had described them — Walker admitted he had placed the recorders there, but had done so with Mayor Bowers' permission[6].

Walker explained he used the recordings to protect himself, should any allegations come against him resulting from the *Morrow vs. City of Tenaha* civil case that was still ongoing at that time.

Although no recording devices were found in the places where the Velcro strips were placed, we did find something equally incriminating. There were two video cameras disguised as smoke detectors located in the City Marshal's Office.

One of the smoke detector cameras was found in a room where periodic city council meetings were held and the other was placed so it looked directly into the office of Barry Washington. It was clear that despite Walker's assertion that he was only covering himself, he and McClure were particularly interested in recording Washington.

It is a federal violation to place hidden recording devices to secretly capture conversations of individuals who do not know they are being recorded. Walker was informed of this and acknowledged he may have violated the law.

Interview of McClure:

As the interviews of Walker and Ford were getting started, Texas Ranger Tom Davis and I pulled up in front of McClure's home in Tenaha. It was a nice, new house built after a previous home on the same property was destroyed by fire.

McClure, who drove a blue Hummer H3, was backing out of his driveway. We pulled up and parked in front of his house. As Davis and I got out of our car, McClure saw us and stopped. We walked toward his car and identified ourselves and indicated we wanted to ask him some questions. He was friendly and said although he was on his way out he would talk with us for a few minutes.

McClure requested we talk in his computer shop and gestured us toward it. He owned a computer repair shop called Computer Clinic, which was located in a small building immediately adjacent to and on the same property as his home. He would later attempt to exploit the location of the computer shop as a technicality in a court motion.

As we sat down in McClure's computer shop, I was struck that it looked

---

[6] This was also denied by Mayor Bowers.

more like an old storage shed than a place of business. The building itself was probably 14 feet long by 10 feet wide. There was a crudely hand-painted sign outside that said "Computer Clinic." There was a wooden floor that was uneven and the place had seen it's better days. It didn't appear to me to be a business that could support the new house and the purchase of a Hummer, nor generate the $1,000-$3,000 weekly cash deposits.

One thing that Tom Davis noted was a sign indicating everything was being recorded. Although we weren't actually being recorded, I came to wish we had been. In fact, I regret that every encounter with McClure was not recorded, because it would have prevented many headaches to come.

As we sat down, I asked McClure if he knew Terrence Ford. McClure acknowledged he knew Ford and they had been friends for several years.

"We traced the Jack Frost extortion letter back to him," I said. "Do you have any idea why he would do that?"

McClure said he didn't know why Ford did it, but indicated he wasn't surprised based on previous dealings he had with Ford.

At this point in the investigation, I had developed some very suspicious findings related to McClure — including the cash deposits, his strange relationship with Fred Walker and the large number of daily phone calls between the two, his association with Ford, the man attempting to extort him, his checkered criminal history, and Walker taking the Marshal's Office surveillance camera hard drives immediately to him before the Rangers arrived at the crime scene.

Despite these suspicious facts however, I still wasn't sure if he had any involvement in the Marshal's Office burglary. I fully believed Walker was involved because it was so apparent the scene was staged, and the way he pushed the Zetas letter and the Brownsville-to-Tenaha map on Ranger Davis seemed like a diversion.

So I began fishing a little bit. I brought up the Marshal's Office burglary and asked some general questions about it.

"Fred brought the hard drives from the surveillance cameras to me to see if I could extract anything useful," he responded. "But they were so damaged I knew it would be impossible to get anything off them."

Our questions then began focusing on Walker and his possible involvement in the burglary.

Even though the questions primarily concerned Walker, McClure must have sensed that Davis and I were suspicious of him as well.

"Do I need a lawyer?" he asked.

"We can't advise you about that one way or the other," I said.

He began expressing disbelief that we implied he was involved in the burglary. But he did not ask for a lawyer or say in any way he wanted the interview to stop. Although it is a technical point, asking "Do I need a lawyer?" and saying "I want a lawyer present" are two different things.

We were under no obligation to read him his Miranda rights, as he was not in custody and we had no intention of arresting him. He was properly told we could not give advice about whether he needed a lawyer and he never indicated he wanted the interview to stop. Far from it — McClure talked incessantly and was always trying to control the conversation. It was clear he wanted to know what we knew.

So at this point, McClure began a pattern that would continue throughout the remainder of the case. He attempted to shift any responsibility or blame to someone else. I later realized McClure was a very astute tactical thinker. He said what he needed to say to get him past the danger of the moment. McClure wasn't a strategic thinker, however. He didn't seem to consider the long-term consequences of short-term explanations and how easy, in many cases, his words might be to disprove.

"I think Barry Washington and Randy Whatley committed the Marshal's Office burglary," he said. "They personally used the money they took in those car stops."

He described a kickback scheme in which local business owners created fake invoices for Washington and Whatley, so their purchases using the seized money appeared legitimate.

But I knew the financial analysis done during the DOJ investigation had shown no apparent incriminating uses of seized money by Washington and Whatley.

Although he was trying his hardest to shift attention to Washington and Whatley, McClure could see Davis and I were not convinced. Then out of nowhere he told us about installing hidden cameras and recording devices in the Tenaha City Hall and the City Marshal's Office for Fred Walker.

McClure claimed Walker was distrustful of Barry Washington and wanted to "cover his ass" from involvement in the *Morrow* case.

McClure said the cameras, disguised as smoke detectors, did not record audio very well. So Walker told him to add voice activated digital recorders in Washington's office and at City Hall. McClure explained he attached the recorders in hidden areas with Velcro and described specifically where the Velcro could be located. He said they were no longer recording anything because Washington had stepped down from his job at the City Marshal's Office.

McClure added that when he and Walker were actively recording, he periodically downloaded the recordings and changed the batteries in the voice activated recorders. McClure even retrieved a digital recorder from within the office while we were talking to show us an example of the type that was used. When we asked him where the recordings were located, McClure said he initially downloaded the recordings, but as time went on, he tired of doing it and showed Walker how to do it. He said some of the recordings were downloaded on Walker's laptop computer.

"I've still got some of the recordings in my house," he said, as he motioned toward his residence.

The interview lasted less than an hour, but we gleaned a lot from it. McClure implicated Walker and himself in an illegal wiretapping scheme. It was clear McClure was doing all he could to divert us from the Marshal's Office burglary. And he succeeded.

It was an example of his tactical thinking. By telling us he possessed recordings derived from an illegal scheme in his house, he unwittingly gave us probable cause for a search warrant. I began drafting an affidavit to present to a federal judge to obtain a search warrant for McClure's home. He had succeeded in moving us momentarily off the Marshal's Office burglary, but inadvertently created a huge problem for himself and a lasting headache for us.

7

IT WAS ALL A JOKE

When I got to work the next morning, Terrence Ford had already called me and left a message. When I called him back, Ford told me he was eager to resolve the situation regarding the Jack Frost letter. I agreed that I also wanted to resolve the situation. I told him it would be better if we met in person and since he was in McKinney, which is close to Dallas, I suggested we meet in the Dallas FBI office the next day.

The Dallas FBI office is located off I-35 near the intersection of Northwest Highway. It is a modern building that could easily pass as the home office of an insurance company.

In the lobby entrance, there is a memorial to all the FBI Agents killed in the line of duty since the agency began in 1908. It's a reminder that we deal with violent people and no matter how routine or mundane the work can be at times, we can never let our guard down or get complacent about our safety.

The day-to-day work of the FBI is far less dangerous than that of a patrol cop who has to react to situations on the street that can turn violent in the blink of an eye.

But the nature of our work is to investigate violations of federal criminal law and that means if we're successful, someone is probably going to jail. I've seen hundreds of different reactions from people when they find their freedom is being taken away. Some are very compliant and resigned to their fate and some resist with violence. The point is you never know how a person might react.

The main thing I knew about Terrence Ford was he sent an extortion letter threatening violence. I could not be certain at that point if he was serious but by bringing him to the FBI office, which has an imposing process for entry, I was giving myself every advantage in case he was.

When Ford arrived, he was very polite and displayed a quiet manner. As the interview started, Ford reiterated what he said two days earlier that the Jack Frost letter was sent to Fred Walker and Rod McClure as a joke.

He described an earlier joke he played on Walker.

"I pretended to be a reporter calling about those interdiction stops shown on CNN," Ford said. "Rod listened in on a three-way connection. I strung Fred along for a few minutes and when I told him it was a joke we all had a good laugh."

Ford said he met McClure in 1993. They had both been DEA informants at the same time.

"We've been at various times very close friends and other times we would barely speak to each other or have no contact at all," he said.

Ford knew Walker through McClure and he believed they were related somehow — possibly cousins.

Ford added, "I'm a screenwriter and I want to develop a screenplay about all the criminal activity going there."

"Have you ever lived in Tenaha?" I asked him.

"No, but I've been there several times visiting Rod," he said.

Ford acknowledged creating both the email address and the post office box referred to in the Jack Frost letter.

He described traveling to Austin with his friend Darla Cabot to open the post office box. I asked him to provide the specific times of his trip to Austin with Cabot. The time they left, arrived in Austin, other stops, etc. His timelines didn't agree with my analysis of his cell phone calls with Cabot. There were two or three calls between the two during the times when Ford said they were together. Now this may have been a simple error in memory on Ford's part, but I took the opportunity to confront him.

"I don't believe you sent the Jack Frost letters as a joke," I said. "It was far too elaborate to be a joke and the point of a joke is ultimately to tell the person about it so you both can have a laugh."

Then I mentioned, without specifically telling him about the inconsistent times of the calls he referenced to Darla Cabot, "There is something you're not telling me and you know what I'm talking about."

Although I was talking about those inconsistent phone call times, he believed I knew a lot more than I did.

Ford slumped and dropped his head as he acknowledged the Jack Frost letters were not sent as a joke.

"It wasn't a joke," he then said. "I was really trying to extort them."

And like so many suspects before him, he thought about a way out.

"I've got very incriminating information on both Rod and Fred but I would like some kind of deal for myself before I tell you," he said.

"I can't make any deals or promises," I responded. "I will have to talk to the prosecuting attorney — her office has that authority."

Ford said he had not been in recent contact with McClure.

"Leave it that way," I said. "At some point maybe we can use you to make recorded phone calls to McClure or Walker to see if they will say anything incriminating." Ford agreed and I told him I would contact him shortly.

After the interview, I quickly called Lisa Flournoy, the Assistant United States Attorney (AUSA) I was working with.

"Lisa, Terrence Ford admitted the Jack Frost letters were a real extortion and he knows a lot of incriminating information about Fred Walker and Rod McClure," I said. "But he wants a deal. I think it would be worth giving him a proffer."

Flournoy agreed we needed to find out what Ford knew and supported doing a proffer. A proffer is a formal interview where the government provides a letter agreeing not to use anything a person says against them in exchange for truthful and complete information. It is not immunity, which is complete protection from prosecution, because under a proffer the person could still be prosecuted for a particular crime if there is independent evidence against them. However, anything they said in a proffer, such as a confession, could not be used against them.

In the case of Ford, we already had a very strong case against him for extortion. Indeed, he confessed to it in a non-custodial interview where no promises had been made to him. So we weren't losing much by offering him the proffer deal. I contacted Ford, who was agreeable to the arrangement, and set up the interview for Friday, August 12, 2011. It was to take place in the United States Attorney's Office in Plano, Texas. Ford mentioned nothing about wanting a lawyer and although he was welcome to bring one, he chose not to.

As it turned out, Lisa Flournoy was not able to attend the Ford proffer due to a scheduling conflict. The United States Attorney for the Eastern District of Texas, Malcolm Bales, a former FBI Agent, agreed to sit in and present the proffer letter to Ford.

Prior to his appointment as U. S. Attorney, Bales was an Assistant U.S. Attorney prosecuting cases out of the Lufkin office which covered Shelby County and Tenaha. He was intimately familiar with the area and its reputation for having corrupt law enforcement so he took a particular interest in this case.

As U. S. Attorney Malcolm Bales, Texas Ranger Tom Davis and I sat down with Ford to begin the interview, we were prepared to hear some incriminating information regarding Fred Walker and Rod McClure. Although it is nice to get information from someone with firsthand knowledge of an illegal scheme, it is not necessarily the end of an investigator's work.

To ensure the person is giving truthful information it sometimes requires a great deal of work to independently corroborate it. Ford would be no different with one big exception. After years of dealing with McClure, Ford learned he needed to protect himself. He had an ace up his sleeve and brought his own corroboration.

8

AN ACE UP THE SLEEVE

Before we began asking Terrence Ford any questions, U. S. Attorney Malcolm Bales presented the proffer letter to him and explained its implications. The person involved in a proffer session is sometimes called "queen for a day" as they can give information, even if it is highly self-incriminating, and not have it used against them if that information is truthful and complete. Ford, again soft spoken and polite, signed the letter.

We began the proffer by asking Ford about the Jack Frost letters. He again went over all the details of establishing an email address, getting Darla Cabot to open the post office box in Austin using his altered insurance cards, drafting the letters themselves and sending them to Walker and McClure.

Ford emphasized Cabot was not aware anything illegal was going on.

"I called her and told her she would likely be contacted by the FBI," he said. "I told her to tell the truth and not worry because I'm the one to blame."

Ford acknowledged he initially lied about sending the letters as a joke and said they were meant for a real extortion because he knew Walker and McClure were making money from the sale of seized narcotics stolen from the Tenaha City Marshal's evidence room.

Ford then began detailing how it all began.

In September 2009, he traveled to McClure's home for the purpose of building deer stands to be used for hunting. At some point on Saturday, September 19, 2009, while working on the deer stands, McClure told Ford the Shelby County Constable's office in Tenaha, which was sitting unmanned due to the resignation of Randy Whatley, had a large amount of drugs stored in its evidence room.

As we later learned, McClure, through his business Computer Clinic, installed the security cameras for both the Tenaha City Marshal's Office and the Constable's Office. He would have been readily familiar with the layout of both offices.

According to Ford, McClure talked him into a plan of breaking into the Constable's Office, stealing the drugs, selling them and making a lot of money. He and McClure then went to the Wal-Mart in Center, Texas, about 10 miles south, where Ford purchased a Crossman 760 Pumpmaster air rifle. Upon their return to Tenaha, Ford and McClure walked the short distance from McClure's home at West Drive and Church Street to the rear entrance of the Constable's Office which faced U.S. Route 59. The entry had two storefront type glass doors likely from a time years ago when the office served as a retail establishment.

Ford said McClure completely shot out the glass doors using the Crossman Pumpmaster. Ford said "When I saw the glass begin to break, I had what I can only describe as a panic attack. Suddenly this silly plot we had been talking about became real and I got scared."

Ford told McClure he no longer wanted any part of it and though McClure balked, they walked together the short distance back to McClure's home. Ford said McClure continued trying to talk him into going back into the Constable's Office and assured him they could get away with it.

Ford said "I just told him I didn't want to do it. I went to bed that night and didn't hear or see anything else."

The next morning, Sunday, September 20, 2009, Ford got up early to deliver the deer stands to the woods to set up for hunting. As he drove by he noticed several Shelby County Sheriff's Office deputies at the Constable's Office.

Ford said "When I saw those Sheriff's cars there I knew Rod must have gone back without me. I called him but he was very coy. Rod told me he wouldn't talk about it with me because I had chickened out."

Ford said McClure later called him and said he learned from Fred Walker that the police had no suspects in the matter. Ford said he never learned from McClure what was stolen from the Constable's Office that night.

He said the next month, October 2009, he traveled to Los Angeles, California to attempt to break into screenwriting.

"I went out to LA to try to break into a screenwriting job and I got a call from Rod."

Apparently emboldened by getting away with breaking into the Constable's

Office, McClure said that he and Fred Walker were going to begin stealing evidentiary narcotics from the City Marshal's Office.

Ford said, "Rod told me Fred was in on it and we could steal the drugs without fear of being caught. He said there was a lot of money to be made by selling the drugs. Even though I needed the money, I turned him down."

Ford and McClure maintained their frequent telephone conversations over the next several months. Ford said once McClure and Walker started the scheme, McClure began bragging to him about how much money he was making selling the evidentiary drugs stolen from the Marshal's Office.

"Rod told me there were hundreds, maybe thousands of pounds of marijuana" Ford said.

McClure told Ford he was splitting the profits evenly with Walker, but Ford didn't believe him.

"If I know Rod like I think I do, he definitely kept more for himself," Ford said.

McClure told Ford he had several individuals helping him sell the drugs. Among them was a man McClure referred to as "Cain" who lived in Shreveport, Louisiana.

"Rod said Cain was a real intimidating guy he used as a bodyguard for a couple of drug deals" Ford said.

Ford said in Tenaha, McClure had two trusted lieutenants who worked for him: Sebastian Ewing and Orlando Padron[7]. Ewing was a Tenaha native a few years younger than McClure.

Padron was a young man from Mexico in the United States illegally. McClure thought of him almost as a son. For example, McClure had "Orlando" tiled into the side wall of his swimming pool along with the first names of his own children. In later testimony at a hearing, McClure referred to Padron as like an "adopted son" to him.

I never learned the reason for the closeness between the two.

Ford said as time went on, his screenwriting efforts failed to produce anything of substance and he began to need money.

"I wasn't having any success with screenwriting and I really was hurting for money," he said. "I had been listening for months to Rod bragging about how much money he was making and I finally relented."

So in approximately May 2010, Ford traveled to Tenaha and got

---

[7] Not their real names.

approximately 14 pounds of marijuana from McClure for the purpose of selling it in the Dallas area.

"Rod had it hidden behind a couch in his computer shop," Ford said. "As I was leaving, Rod said he was going to meet his girlfriend Amy."

Ford didn't know Amy's last name. We later identified her as Amy Johnson[8] and she became one of the key witnesses in the case.

When Ford returned to McKinney, he attempted to sell the marijuana he got from McClure in the Oak Cliff section of Dallas. Whatever Ford's talents in the world were, they were not in drug dealing.

On the two occasions he attempted selling marijuana, he was ripped off both times. On the second attempt, not only was his marijuana stolen but his wallet as well. Angered at this, Ford actually called the Dallas police.

"I was so mad that they would take my wallet, I called the police," Ford said.

When they arrived, he detailed getting his wallet stolen and gave details about the thieves but didn't mention the marijuana. It was a small but important way we could corroborate some of his story because there would be a police report documenting the place, date and time.

Ford didn't know exactly when Walker and McClure began stealing marijuana from the Marshal's Office evidence room but as he learned from his frequent conversations with McClure, it was ongoing for months.

To hide the missing marijuana, McClure described to Ford of using fire starter bricks to replace what was stolen.

The fire starter bricks, used to start campfires, were coincidentally of the same shape and weight as that used by some drug traffickers to package and transport marijuana.

In one of his interdiction stops, Barry Washington had seized over 400 pounds of marijuana which was packaged in brick form. It was from this seizure that McClure and Walker primarily stole during the months before the staged burglary, because it could be easily replaced by the fire starter bricks and not raise suspicion that anything was missing.

Walker and McClure weren't concerned the marijuana would ever be needed for trial because of District Attorney Lynda K. Russell's slowness or non-action in prosecuting any of the Tenaha cases.

Ford said he and McClure had many conversations about the ongoing

---

[8] Not her real name.

theft of drugs from the Marshal's Office.

"I told Rod that if anyone tested those fire starter bricks it would quickly be apparent it wasn't marijuana," Ford said.

In addition, Ford said the bricks did not have the distinctive smell of marijuana and that could be suspicious over time.

"Rod didn't care one bit about anyone getting suspicious until Fred decided to run for Constable," he said. "He knew that a new City Marshal would come in and likely inventory the evidence room and the phony fire starter bricks would be found."

McClure told Ford that he thought Walker could serve as both City Marshal and Constable but later found out he could not do both. That meant a new City Marshal would be hired. In addition, Ford said Walker had repeatedly asked District Attorney Russell for destruction orders for the narcotics associated with the Tenaha cases. This would have made things easy because Walker could just say he destroyed the drugs — because the DA authorized it — since they weren't going to be used in any prosecutions. But Russell never produced the destruction orders.

Based on the concerns about a new incoming City Marshal, Ford said McClure formulated a plan to stage a burglary at the Marshal's Office to cover up the ongoing marijuana theft.

Ford said "Rod had this idea to direct suspicion for the burglary to the Zetas drug cartel. He learned from Fred that a fingerprint had been found on some plastic wrapping used to conceal some marijuana that had been seized by Barry Washington."

Indeed, we later confirmed that a fingerprint lifted from the plastic wrapping in a seizure of over 400 pounds of marijuana had been linked through laboratory analysis to an individual associated with the Zetas. To exploit this and cast suspicion elsewhere, McClure told Ford he would have his girlfriend, Amy Johnson, write a letter in Spanish, to be left at the crime scene, which would appear to be from the Zetas. McClure felt this would lead investigators to conclude the Zetas had returned to Tenaha to reclaim their seized marijuana.

McClure told Ford he planned to destroy the hard drives connected to the surveillance cameras so there would be no recorded digital evidence of what really happened. Ironically, McClure subsequently got a contract from the City of Tenaha for $13,000 to replace the hard drives he destroyed in staging the burglary.

During the week beginning Monday, August 16, 2010, Barry Washington left Tenaha to attend a law enforcement seminar in New Orleans. Over the course of that week, Walker and McClure planned and carried out the staging of the Marshal's Office burglary. As I would later find, Walker and McClure had to operate around Washington. This was the actual motivation behind the secret wiretapping of his office, to find something incriminating which could be used to force him to resign.

Ford said after the staging of the burglary, McClure texted him a series of pictures of marijuana, pills and cocaine which were stolen from the Marshal's Office. Again tempted by the lure of easy money and after months of bragging by McClure of how much money was being made, Ford traveled to Tenaha to get more marijuana and this time, pills, to sell. Probably because he knew Ford was such an ineffective drug dealer, McClure refused to front him any cocaine.

It was an incredible story. But if we were going to use Ford as a witness, his story would not be enough. We had to independently corroborate as much as we could. The easiest way to start this process is to ask the person being interviewed if they know of any independent evidence to prove their story.

So I asked the question, "Do you know any way we can independently verify what you're telling us is true?"

Ford didn't immediately answer but simply pulled out his cell phone.

"I've known Rod McClure long enough to know that I had to protect myself and I had a feeling this was all going to come out one way or the other and he would probably blame me so I gave myself a little insurance policy," he said.

Ford showed us the texts and accompanying photos of the drugs McClure had sent him as an enticement. Ranger Tom Davis and I could barely believe what we were seeing. Ford had actually saved the texts and photos. Having already gone through a lengthy analysis of phone records, I knew the cell phone number sending the photos and text messages was McClure's. The text messages were as follows:

9 kilos of coke
Hydro's yellow 10/325 qty 200
2mg Xanax qty 730
Hydro's blue 10/500 have 2215
Hydro's 10/650 green 950
Got 480 somas
3895 XO's need to get rid of

Each of these separate text messages had an accompanying photograph that appeared to be accurately described by the text. For example, a photograph of a bag of a white powdery substance was described as "9 kilos of coke." The remaining texts, for those unfamiliar, were referring to the prescription drugs: Hydrocodone, a pain killer; Xanax (alprazolam), an anxiety drug; Soma (carisoprodol), a muscle relaxant; and Ecstasy (MDMA), a psychoactive drug.

We knew from the Texas Department of Public Safety (DPS) lab labels found on empty boxes in the Marshal's Office evidence room that the amounts McClure listed in the texts, although not an exact match, were close to the amounts of missing prescription drugs. The nine kilos of cocaine, a large amount of narcotics, was not a part of any of the missing drugs known to have been in the evidence room.

In addition to the text/photos, Ford also had two other photos sent to him from McClure that showed what appeared to be a large amount of marijuana.

In one of the photos, three large marijuana bricks were sitting on a workbench. The other photo was of leafy marijuana spread out and fully covering a pool table.

In the photo with the marijuana bricks, an old door with chipped paint was visible behind the work bench. In the other photo, a Coke machine was clearly behind the pool table. I recalled seeing the Coke machine in a series of photos obtained from the city owned laptop computer turned over to current Tenaha City Marshal Tom Reader from Fred Walker.

The Coke machine was inside an unattached garage on McClure's property. We later confirmed the door with the chipped paint in the other photograph was also in the same unattached garage.

It was a good start toward corroborating Ford's statement. The texts and photos were particularly incriminating for McClure. But McClure wasn't the main target. This case was about public corruption. We wanted to get evidence against Fred Walker, the public official.

Tom Davis said "It surely gets us a case against McClure but there's nothing incriminating about Walker except what McClure told him."

He was right. So far, the only evidence we had against Walker was circumstantial and third hand. Ford had no direct contact with Walker, either in person, telephonically or otherwise, that involved anything illegal. Everything Ford knew about Walker's illegal activity came through his conversations with McClure. Ford would not be able to testify about hearsay.

So we pondered where to go with this new information. I completed the affidavit for a search warrant at McClure's home for evidence of illegal wiretapping and we planned to execute the warrant the next Monday, August

15, 2011.

Although I considered the search warrant and McClure's allegations of wiretapping City Hall and the Marshal's Office more of a distraction, perhaps it might reveal incriminating evidence against Fred Walker. We already had his confession about the wiretapping, but without corroborating evidence, a prosecution would be unlikely.

Before our interview with Ford ended, we asked him if there was anything else we needed to know or that we had not asked him about.

"I've got another picture of Rod although it wasn't meant to be a picture of him." He showed us another photo on his phone.

This one showed a gun cabinet with several rifles, a bulletproof vest, and a hand grenade. The cabinet had a glass front. When the picture was taken, the flash of the camera caught the image of the person taking the photo reflected in the glass front. The person taking the photo was Rod McClure.

Ford said "That was taken in Rod's house and he likely still has all those guns — despite being a felon."

The information prompted me to call in ATF Special Agent Blaine Gillis on the chance the guns were at McClure's residence when we conducted the search warrant. ATF Agents are experts regarding guns, and one of the primary violations they investigate is felon in possession of a firearm.

Because Ford wasn't certain when the photo had been taken, I decided not to amend the search warrant to include guns. If McClure still had them and they were in plain sight, we could seize them under the plain view doctrine, which allows officers to seize evidence of crime without a search warrant when that evidence is in plain sight. Gillis would be the best person to have along at the search warrant if guns were found.

9

A HOUSE FULL OF GUNS

It was hot the day we executed the search warrant at Rod McClure's home in Tenaha on Monday August 15, 2011. There were five FBI Agents, three Texas Rangers, and one ATF Agent. Also present was Shelby County Constable Stanley Burgay.

To the general public this might seem like an excessive number of people. However, the execution of search warrants, even on seemingly routine, non-violent cases, can be unpredictable and can present danger at any time. So it is a customary practice to have enough people on hand should there be more people present in the home than usual at the time of the warrant.

Some people become very angry and emotional when law enforcement officers enter their home. I can understand the reaction. Any person will have some type of emotional response to having their home searched. Having enough officers and agents present allows control of those people who sometimes cannot control their emotions. It is as much for their safety as it is the safety of the officers to have ample manpower at a search warrant.

We knocked on McClure's front door. He opened the door and we pulled him outside onto the front porch. He was placed in handcuffs[9] and told a search warrant was being executed at his home. Several Agents and Rangers

---

[9] Placing someone in handcuffs at the beginning of a search warrant is done to ensure safety until control of the residence is established. It does not mean someone is under arrest but rather they are momentarily detained for safety reasons. Once their level of compliance is determined, they are uncuffed and usually asked to remain seated in a certain area of the home. However, if they choose to do so, they may leave the residence while the search is being conducted.

immediately entered the home to ensure no one else was present and to mitigate any potential threats.

While the home was being cleared, McClure was highly flustered and kept asking "What is this about? I haven't done anything, what is this about?"

His response was not unusual or unreasonable. However, my focus was on ensuring the other Agents and Rangers cleared the home first. As I stood with him, I told him I would answer his questions momentarily.

When the house was cleared and no others found to be present, we led McClure into the house while preparing to conduct the search. During the initial phase of a search warrant, the layout of the house is assessed, if not known previously, and photographs are taken before anything is touched. This is done to document the condition of the house and its contents. Upon entering the house, I immediately noticed the gun cabinet from the photograph shown to me by Ford. It appeared to contain the same rifles, bulletproof vest, and hand grenade seen in the Ford photograph.

ATF Agent Gillis said, "It looks like I've got my work cut out for me. I'll start inventorying the guns."

While this was happening, I walked out to the unattached garage and took a photo of the Coke machine seen in the picture McClure sent to Ford with the marijuana spread over the pool table. The pool table was no longer in the garage.

I went back into the main house. With the search now underway, Ranger Tom Davis and I brought McClure into the dining room. FBI Agent Terry Lane, a classmate of mine from New Agent's Training at the FBI Academy who was assigned in Lufkin, Texas, also sat down with us. We took his handcuffs off and asked him if he was interested in answering some questions. He was still very animated and he kept saying this was all a mistake and a misunderstanding.

Unlike our previous interview of McClure, we were not guests in his home. Under the authority to conduct a search warrant, Agents control access to the home or business being searched. So McClure could not simply ask us to leave, and although he was not under arrest he was not free to move about his home for safety reasons. He was told he could leave if he wished — but if he remained, he would have to remain seated in the dining room and his movements would be controlled.

In addition, finding guns in his home raised the possibility of a probable cause arrest. This is an arrest done without a warrant when the facts and circumstances of a situation lead an Officer or Agent to reasonably conclude that a crime has been committed. It is a common thing for local and state

Officers, but somewhat rare in federal law enforcement.

Also, most of the time when a search warrant is conducted, persons in the place being searched are routinely interviewed, although they are under no requirement to consent. In this instance, McClure was the only person in the home, he was suspected of involvement in illegal wiretapping, and was a convicted felon seemingly in possession of several guns.

The Miranda warning of a person's right to silence is required when a person is questioned while in custody. The determination of when a person is in custody can sometimes be subjective. In this case with numerous law enforcement officials in his home restricting his movement, it would not have been unreasonable for McClure to assume he was in custody.

If he made any incriminating statements, I wanted to ensure they would be admissible in court. For that reason, and as difficult as it was to get a word in edgewise with him, I told him before we began asking him questions, he would need to be read his Miranda rights and agree to waive them.

Normally I kept a standard form titled Advice of Rights which listed each of a person's Constitutional rights under Miranda, the 1966 Supreme Court case ensuring a person is advised of their rights to silence and to have an attorney present prior to questioning while in custody.

The form has a signature line acknowledging they've read, understand and are waiving their rights. On this day, of all days however, I didn't have the form in the portfolio notebook I routinely carried. I inadvertently failed to replace it after the last time I used one. All we had was a card Tom Davis carried with him that listed the Miranda rights. Davis read McClure the Miranda rights from the card. McClure acknowledged his rights and agreed to waive them and submit to questioning. Unfortunately we didn't have him sign anything. This would be another huge headache down the road.

Some readers may be asking at this point why the interview with McClure was not recorded. At that time, it was a long standing policy in the FBI that interviews were not recorded. This goes back to the days of J. Edgar Hoover, the legendary Director of the FBI from 1924 to 1972.

The FBI has always been slow to embrace change, especially in technology. Despite a public perception that we have instant access to the latest technology, much of our work is conducted with very low tech methods.

There is a saying in the FBI: "Yesterday's technology — tomorrow". For instance, when air conditioning became a standard feature in cars in the 1960s, Mr. Hoover ordered the air conditioning systems of FBI cars to be removed. Why? Maybe it was some mythological belief that FBI Agents didn't need air conditioning or maybe because it was new technology he didn't trust. I suppose he felt the administrative system he established in 1924 and the technology available at the time had served the FBI well and was good enough. Even though he died in 1972, Hoover's influence and his reluctance to embrace change is still, in many ways, part of the FBI.

For reasons that will become clear to the reader, I regret that every encounter with Rod McClure was not audio and video recorded. Although there is a new policy that requires all custodial interviews to be recorded, there still is no requirement that routine, non-custodial interviews, even those of investigative targets, be recorded.

My objective in interviewing McClure that day was to gather any information he knew about Fred Walker being involved in illegal activity.

In other words, I wanted ultimately to have McClure as a cooperating witness. We already had very strong incriminating evidence against him for numerous violations. However, before anyone can be an effective witness, their own wrongdoing must be acknowledged, otherwise their credibility can be shredded by a good defense attorney when they take the stand to testify.

To assess how truthful McClure was going to be, I started the interview by showing him the picture I had just taken of the Coke machine in his garage and asked him what it was.

He said "That's the Coke machine out in my garage."

I next showed him the texted photograph of the marijuana on the pool table with his Coke machine clearly visible behind it that I obtained from Terrence Ford. It was one of the few times I saw McClure at a loss for words. He knew he was caught and yet we could tell the wheels in his mind were spinning fast. I'm sure he was running through his mind how on earth I could have obtained this photo.

McClure acknowledged "That's marijuana".

He then gave three different explanations of how and why it was there.

First, he said, "It came from the Marshal's Office and was a payment for teaching someone how to disable security cameras."

The next explanation was, "It belongs to an individual who sold marijuana for Newton Johnson (Shelby County Sheriff)."

Finally, McClure said, "Barry Washington gave the marijuana to me as payment for telling him about the hidden surveillance cameras in the Marshal's Office."

He could see with each explanation that we didn't believe him. He even threw out the names of several DEA Agents he had worked with back in the

1990s who would vouch for him. Next, in the same way he previously threw us off with the wiretapping information, he alleged former Constable Randy Whatley was a marijuana dealer. Again, we weren't buying it. For the next couple of hours, we went back and forth with him. Although he ultimately admitted staging the burglary, having his girlfriend write the Spanish language Zetas letter, conducting the Constable's Office burglary, he kept insisting Fred Walker wasn't in on any of it.

The interesting thing I noticed about McClure was although he talked constantly, he was clearly and intently thinking of something else and trying to steer the conversation. Evidence of his desire or need to control a conversation can be found during a later court hearing before United States Magistrate Judge Keith Giblin. During the hearing Judge Giblin said:

Q: Now do you generally understand the charges against you?

A: Um —

Q: Don't make any statements about it, now, because I want to make sure that you-- that before you make statements, that you visit with your lawyer, okay? I just want to - do you understand what you're charged with?

A: Yes sir, that the charge —

Q: Okay, don't say — don't — I know you want to talk to me about the original charge. And again, I'm not being rude to you, Mr. McClure. I just don't want you to make a statement because I can't do anything about this. I, you know, this is for the trial judge to figure out and your lawyer to —

A: All right. I'm saying — no, no, no. I'm not even talking about that. I'm talking about what they said I went to prison for, that charge is incorrect. That's what —

Q: Okay

A: (indiscernible)

Q: Okay. Well I —

A: Yeah, I understand everything else.

Q: Yeah. I just want to make sure. Again, I'm trying to protect your rights. I just don't want you to blurt out anything until your lawyer's —

A: Don't worry.

McClure even interrupted the Judge when he was being told not to blurt anything out. Our interview with him was no different. McClure wanted to control it and constantly interrupted. He never asked for a lawyer or refused to answer questions, as both rights had been explained to him. It was as if he was stalling us, confident that he could send us down another path.

Finally, he seemed to drop his shoulders a little and the thinking stopped and he simply said "Fred did it."

"He planned and participated in the whole thing," McClure said.

During the course of our interview with McClure, the search warrant was ongoing. ATF Agent Gillis catalogued thirteen guns and hundreds of rounds of various types of ammunition. Most of the guns were hunting rifles and shotguns. One of the rifles was an AK-47 style assault rifle. There was also a two-shot derringer. McClure also had a ballistic vest. The hand grenade seen in the Ford photograph turned out to be a replica.

As the search warrant itself was based on illegal wiretapping and authorized us to take computers and related media, we seized several hard drives, thumb drives, laptop computers, and cell phones.

I called Prosecutor Lisa Flournoy and told her we found a large number of guns in addition to the computers we were seizing. Knowing McClure's criminal history, which included shooting his cousin with a handgun, she said "We can't ignore the fact that he has all those guns."

She recommended we arrest him for felon in possession of a firearm based on the plain sight evidence of the guns. McClure was placed under arrest and transported to the Angelina County jail.

10

THE RIDE TO BEAUMONT

The next day, August 16, 2011, the ATF filed a criminal complaint against McClure with the federal district court in Beaumont, Texas for Felon in Possession of a Firearm. A criminal complaint is a formal filing with a court usually done when a warrantless arrest is conducted. An affidavit accompanies it setting out the probable cause for the arrest.

A preliminary hearing is required within ten days of an arrest based on a complaint unless the case is presented to a grand jury within that time. It only took a day as Lisa Flournoy presented the matter to the Grand Jury on August 17, 2011.

The Grand Jury issued what is known as a true bill indictment, formally charging McClure.

After an indictment, the person being charged is entitled to a hearing known in the federal system as an initial appearance before a United States Magistrate Judge. This is a formal hearing where the person is advised of the charges against them, a determination is made of their ability to afford a lawyer, and whether or not the person will be detained pending trial.

Lisa Flournoy and I discussed how McClure's arrest would affect the ongoing public corruption investigation. We both agreed the wiretapping allegations and finding him in possession of guns in his home were separate issues from the drug trafficking associated with the staged Marshal's Office burglary.

Since the Felon in Possession matter seemed obvious and clear cut, Lisa said "my strategy is to get it adjudicated and out of the way and continue the main investigation."

The drug trafficking still involved corroborating Terrence Ford's statement, locating McClure's girlfriend Amy Johnson, author of the Zetas letter, finding "Cain" and the other dealers McClure used, but most importantly, finding direct incriminating evidence of Fred Walker's involvement.

It seemed like a perfectly reasonable strategy, as the gun case evolved from McClure's red herring about wiretapping. But this simple decision to get the gun case out of the way would later unwittingly allow McClure an avenue to exploit a technical point and nearly get the entire case thrown out.

Because McClure was being held in the Angelina County jail, it was necessary to transport him to the Magistrate's court in Beaumont, 110 miles away, for his initial appearance.

Normally this would be a routine task with minimal conversation between the transporting Agents/Officers and the arrestee. And any conversation would be incidental and unrelated to anything regarding the arrestee's case. Like most things in this case however, nothing was routine about this transport.

To backtrack a moment, the Angelina County Jail where McClure was initially detained was the closest jail that accepted federal prisoners. When he arrived, he was told he could not make any telephone calls and was not allowed any calls during his first night there. I don't know where this order came from but I quickly reversed it. McClure then made calls to his mother and his wife.

At the conclusion of our interview with him during the search warrant at his home, we seemed to be in agreement with McClure that he wanted to cooperate and help us against Fred Walker.

To follow up, Ranger Tom Davis, FBI Agent Terry Lane and I went to see McClure in jail the next day, August 16, 2011. But after a night in jail with no telephone calls any cooperation he planned to give was gone.

He was belligerent, and said in no uncertain terms "I have absolutely nothing to say to you."

As we were preparing to leave, McClure became confrontational and made a couple of steps toward Lane who pushed him back. McClure backed down and we left with no illusions that he would be cooperating.

To transport McClure to his initial appearance the next day, August 17, 2011, Davis and Lane went by the jail to pick him up for the two hour drive to Beaumont. They had no intentions of questioning him or expectations that a word would be spoken based on his demeanor the day before. But after another night in jail, McClure's tactics changed again. Now he wanted to talk.

When Davis and Lane first arrived at the jail for the transport, McClure complained of having a headache. He told them "I had a stroke a few years ago and developed a routine of taking baby aspirin. If I don't take the baby aspirin I get headaches."

Davis and Lane agreed to stop and get him some baby aspirin on the way out of town.

Prior to departing the jail however, McClure requested to smoke a cigarette borrowed from a jailer.

Lane asked, "Is smoking a cigarette the best idea for someone who had a stroke?"

"Other than the headache, I'm in good health," McClure said. Gone was the belligerent attitude from the day before.

After departing the jail, a quick stop was made to get the baby aspirin for McClure. They bought him a bottle of water to go with the aspirin. As they started the trip to Beaumont, McClure started by saying "I wish this case was over already and I'm ready to move forward."

Davis and Lane cautioned him about making any statements but McClure was adamant he wanted to talk.

Unfortunately this is another instance where an audio recording would have prevented a lot of problems to come. McClure was told if he wanted to talk he would have to first waive his Miranda rights. He said he already waived them but out of caution, Davis read McClure his rights from the same pre-printed card he read to him two days earlier. McClure, who could hardly be contained, verbally acknowledged his rights and waived them.

McClure's 2nd Confession:

McClure said the "original idea of stealing and selling the drugs from the Marshal's Office was Walker's plan."

McClure said he developed a network of dealers and acted as an intermediary. He denied directly selling the stolen drugs he obtained from Walker but relied on the dealers. Among the dealers McClure named were Terrence Ford, Sebastian Ewing, Orlando Padron, a cousin nicknamed "Buddy,"[10] Dan Ulman,[11] "Big Brian" and "Cain". McClure claimed he did not know Cain's real name but he sold drugs for him in Shreveport. He also did not know Big Brian's real name.

---

[10] Not his real name.

[11] Not his real name.

McClure admitted breaking into the Constable's Office in 2009 with Terrence Ford and stealing about 20 pounds of marijuana.

"It was after the actual burglary of the Constable's Office that Walker proposed the idea of stealing the drugs in the Marshal's Office," he said.

McClure acknowledged the subsequent burglary of the Marshal's Office was planned and staged to cover up the ongoing theft of drugs.

"Walker wanted to run for Constable but was afraid that after he left the City Marshal job that an inventory of the evidence room would reveal the scheme," he said.

Also, Walker had been unsuccessful in obtaining destruction orders for the drug evidence from District Attorney Lynda K. Russell and this was the final impetus for the staged burglary..

McClure said that in addition to marijuana, he and Walker also removed a large amount of prescription and illegal pills such as Ecstasy, Xanex, Hydrocodone, and Somas. He said he had put the various types of pills into plastic bags and took pictures of each bag.

McClure admitted having a woman named Amy Johnson write the Spanish-language letter conveniently recovered at the scene by Walker, to make it appear the Zetas cartel had conducted the burglary. He also said the Mapquest printout with the route from Brownsville to Tenaha had been printed out in the Marshal's Office and left behind as an additional false clue hinting at the Zetas.

Because there were a large number of seized handguns which were in the evidence room along with the drugs, McClure said Walker felt it would not be believable that Mexican drug cartel members would break into an evidence room and simply leave handguns there.

McClure could not recall the specific number of handguns involved but he added that one of them was the gun he used to shoot his cousin, Cecil Moss, in 1995. McClure said he and Walker drove south of Tenaha and disposed of the guns off a bridge over Flat Fork Creek.

One the great concerns in corruption cases involving police officers is what to do when it comes time to arrest them. It has to be assumed that police officers are armed at all times. They are well trained in the use of firearms and tactics.

Charges of corruption can be psychologically devastating, because the officer has likely spent a career building a reputation of being upstanding and on the right side of the law. The public shame can cause irrational and unpredictable behavior.

Because of this concern, McClure was asked if Walker had any violent tendencies.

"Walker doesn't have a violent personality but one time told me that two of my dealers, Dan Ulman and Big Brian, would likely have to be killed at some point because of the risk of their talking to police if they were caught on other charges," McClure said.

Why Walker considered only Ulman and Big Brian a threat to talk to police if caught on other charges and not Terrence Ford, Sebastian Ewing, and Orlando Padron I never found out.

This revelation caused me to reconsider that the January 2010 suicide of David Thompson, McClure's friend who was into child pornography and whose death was solely investigated by Fred Walker after Thompson had been visited by the Secret Service, was not necessarily a suicide.

It would have been bad for Walker and McClure for Thompson to reveal what he might have known to the Secret Service. If what McClure said was true about Walker contemplating the need to kill Ulman and Big Brian[12], it wasn't a huge leap to consider he would want Thompson out of the way as well.

With the circumstantial evidence I had seen so far that indicated Walker was also part of a staged burglary, a staged suicide didn't seem that outrageous.

My suspicion that Thompson's death may not have been a suicide only grew a few days after McClure's arrest, when I received a call from a local defense attorney who said he had been visited by a Constable.

The attorney didn't name the Constable but said he might have been involved in a murder and may need representation. The attorney wanted to know if any such charges were going to be filed. I simply said there was an ongoing investigation and if his potential client wanted to cooperate, now would be a good time to begin. I never heard back from the attorney.

When we ended the interview of McClure at his house on August 15, 2011, he had agreed to cooperate against Walker.

The next day in the jail, he was belligerent and said he had no intention of cooperating.

The day after that, he initiated and gave a full confession while being transported to his initial appearance on the felon in possession charge.

---

[12] Through no lack of effort, we were never able to identify Big Brian. There were several individuals names Brian, who were involved in narcotics, but we were never able to distinguish which one he might have been.

I have no explanation for his flip flops other than as I later learned, McClure was constantly plotting how best to exploit any situation to his advantage.

My opinion is he was thinking short term and was focused solely on getting out of jail. By providing a confession on the ride to his initial appearance, McClure must have believed the Magistrate would not detain him pending trial. By being out of jail, he would be able to coordinate and control the potential testimony of witnesses against him.

As it turned out though, his strategy didn't work. Prosecutor Lisa Flournoy asked for detention and the Magistrate set a hearing for two days later on August 19, 2011.

A detention hearing is held when the government believes a defendant is either a danger to the community or a flight risk. Evidence is presented by both sides and the Magistrate decides if the defendant is detained pending trial or released on a bond.

McClure was appointed an attorney from the United States Public Defender's Office to represent him in the detention hearing.

Lisa Flournoy began planning for the detention hearing and told me I would be the sole government witness.

11

FLAT FORK CREEK

To follow up on information provided to us by McClure during his transport from Lufkin to Beaumont for the initial appearance, Texas Ranger Tom Davis contacted the Department of Public Safety (DPS) Dive Team to attempt to recover the guns stolen from the Marshal's Office evidence room that McClure said were thrown into a creek.

Flat Fork Creek winds its way throughout Shelby County on its way to the gigantic Toledo Bend Reservoir separating Texas from Louisiana. It is fairly wide where it goes under a bridge on Highway 96, approximately eight miles south of Tenaha. McClure had described throwing several handguns off the east side of the Highway 96 bridge.

In 2010, when this was done, the creek level was relatively full. However, by the late summer of 2011, one of the worst droughts in Texas history had driven the creek level to just a few inches in places.

To begin planning their dive, the DPS divers walked onto the bridge to assess where to best enter the creek. Because of the low water level, a pistol was clearly visible on the shallow creek bottom just beneath the bridge.

Terry Lane, my classmate from Quantico, observed, "Well this is gonna be easy. There's one of the guns right there."

As it turned out, the creek was so low that the DPS divers never had to use their scuba equipment. They conducted the search by simply following a shoulder to shoulder grid pattern on their hands and knees and feeling the creek bottom as they went along.

Seven handguns were recovered that day. Also found were two sledgehammers which were likely used to bust up the doors of the Marshal's Office and destroy the computer hard drives that stored surveillance camera footage of what actually happened.

One gun known to be missing from the evidence room was a Ruger .22. The pistol seen in the shallow water from the bridge turned out to be the Ruger. Another of the recovered guns was the same one used by McClure when he shot and wounded his cousin in 1995.

Finding the guns exactly where McClure said they would be with two of them known to have been stored in the evidence room was strong corroboration of his confession. Another indication of his confession's overall truthfulness was that much of what was offered was consistent with Terrence Ford's previous statement.

Although McClure tried to make it to appear that Fred Walker was the mastermind of all things criminal in Tenaha, I was beginning to believe that McClure was the master manipulator who likely had long ago compromised Walker into providing him protection from law enforcement.

One of the things Ford told us about McClure was he was very charming when he wanted to be and "hellbent on having everyone being his flunky."

Nothing I had seen up to this point contradicted Ford's assertion.

After recovering the guns from Flat Fork Creek, Tom Davis, Terry Lane and I located and interviewed Amy Johnson, the woman Ford and McClure told us had written the Spanish-language Zetas letter recovered by Walker at the staged burglary. Johnson was separated from her husband when she started an intimate relationship with McClure, around February 2010.

Johnson told us she and McClure traveled several times to gambling casinos in Shreveport, Louisiana and stayed together in hotels associated with the casinos.

Johnson said McClure told her Fred Walker had an uncle who was recently deceased. To get the bulk of the uncle's estate, McClure told her Walker agreed to pay him $6,000 to falsely testify that Walker had been the uncle's primary caregiver to contest other family members seeking a portion of the uncle's assets. We would later learn McClure did benefit from Walker's uncle's estate when our financial analysis revealed Walker used a big part of it to pay McClure's legal expenses.

Johnson acknowledged writing the Zetas letter.

"Rod asked me to do it as a joke but he didn't tell me any details," she said. "My mother was fluent in Spanish and I can easily understand the spoken language, but I'm not very good at written Spanish."

Johnson added, "Rod had already written a letter in English and I used an English to Spanish dictionary to translate it."

Johnson appeared to be visibly upset when she learned the letter had been found at the scene of the Marshal's Office burglary. She was emphatic that McClure had told her the letter was a joke and did not mention anything about it being used as part of a staged burglary.

We also learned from Johnson that while in Shreveport with McClure at some point in the late spring or early summer of 2010, she met "Cain" outside the Sam's Town casino. Johnson said "I didn't know his real name but they definitely knew each other."

I subsequently learned through telephone records analysis that Cain was Kenneth McCaney[13], a native of Shreveport who had drug charges pending against him in Louisiana. We began preparations to contact him in coordination with the prosecutors handling his case.

---

[13] Not his real name.

12

310 WEST DRIVE

McClure's detention hearing was held on Friday, August 19, 2011 in the Beaumont court room of Magistrate Judge Keith Giblin. Several members of McClure's family were present in the courtroom to support him.

Lisa Flournoy called me to the stand. I testified to the overall investigation and that we had unexpectedly come across the wiretapping allegations made by McClure, which in turn led to the search warrant at his home where we found the 13 guns he was possessing illegally.

My testimony touched on a couple of incidents in McClure's criminal history, the shooting of his cousin and an attempted sexual assault, which indicated he had acted with violence in the past.

Finally, Flournoy asked me about concerns of evidence being destroyed if McClure were released. I testified I had such concerns primarily based on McClure's own admission during his transport from Angelina County that he and Walker had destroyed the recorders used in bugging Barry Washington's office and City Hall, after initially telling us about them on August 8.

Next I was cross-examined by McClure's appointed counsel, John McElroy. His questions were clearly aimed at establishing two points: That I had put the wrong address for McClure's residence in the search warrant and the pictures I had of him with a hunting rifle were from a stolen laptop.

In the course of two days McClure had gone from saying he wanted the whole thing over and giving a full confession, to now trying to exploit technical arguments.

As McElroy had just met with McClure, it was clear he was going on what he had been told by McClure rather than independent investigation.

He asked me: Do you remember whether there was an address that was indicated on the search warrant?

A. Yes sir, there was.

Q. Was it for his house or some other location?

A. It was for his house.

Q. Do you understand that his business is a different address?

A. I do not know that it's a different address.

Q. If it is a different address would you agree with me that the search warrant was ineffective as to the search of that address — or that business?

A. I really couldn't comment on that.

Although I couldn't recall it immediately on the stand, I later looked at the photographs we took of the residence and his computer shop the day of the search warrant. The residence clearly had a nice brass plaque with the number 310 near the front door.

The computer shop did not have any visible address markings. In my search warrant affidavit, I had listed McClure's residence as 310 West Drive. McElroy tried to get me to acknowledge that if I had put the wrong address in the search warrant, that would render it ineffective. This issue would resurface at a subsequent hearing.

Next, McElroy questioned me about the glass doors on McClure's gun cabinet. I thought he was leading to a question about Ford's photograph, in which McClure's image had inadvertently been captured by the flash of the camera while taking a picture of the guns.

However, his next question was about the photograph of McClure holding a hunting rifle. This photo came from the Marshal's Office laptop turned over by Fred Walker to Tom Reader who had it forensically analyzed. He tried his best to get me to say the laptop had been stolen. McElroy asked me: You said when you went into the house you found a gun cabinet with several firearms in it?

A. Correct.

Q. Was the gun cabinet locked or unlocked?

A. Unlocked.

Q. What type of cabinet — did it have any glass doors or —

A. Yes sir.

Q. You indicated there was a photograph of Mr. McClure holding a firearm. Where did that photograph come from?

A. It was from a computer that was turned over to us and the files of that computer were obtained.

Q. You mean that were stolen?

A. No.

Q. The computer had been stolen, correct?

A. No.

Q. You don't believe that's correct?

A. No.

McClure would later accuse me of lying about where I obtained the hunting rifle photograph, by mistakenly conflating my testimony about the glass doors — not realizing his own attorney had neglected to distinguish between the two photographs in his questioning of me.

In his final questions to me, McElroy asked me if McClure was cooperating with the investigation, as a way — I assume — to establish to the court what a good guy he was. At that point, I believed he was cooperating, based on his full confession two days before.

Q: Ms. Flournoy indicated that he has been cooperative since — somewhat cooperative since he's been arrested, is that correct?

A. Yes sir.

Q. He talked to you?

A. Yes sir.

Q. And you said he talked to two other Agents?

A. Yes sir.

Q. When he found out that you were looking for him he didn't run, did he?

A. No, he did not.

McElroy was trying to establish that McClure was cooperative and not a threat or a flight risk. But based on his overall questioning of me, it was looking like McClure's cooperation was once again wavering.

After my testimony, McElroy continued trying to establish McClure wasn't a flight risk or a danger to the community by calling his wife, Betsy Smith[14]. During cross examination, Lisa Flournoy got Betsy to acknowledge

---

[14] Not her real name.

he was a felon who could not legally have guns. In following up on a question, McElroy asked me about McClure not being arrested in the last few years.

Flournoy asked her: Now, your husband has not been arrested in the last several years?

A. No ma'am.

Q. Has he been in any trouble with the law?

A. No ma'am — no ma'am.

Q. Would you consider Constable Fred Walker to be his best friend?

A. I wouldn't say — he's a cousin, I mean.

Q. He's a close friend, isn't he?

A. He's a — yeah.

Q. I mean, you all have gone on cruises together, you hang out socially?

A. Yes ma'am.

Q. So would you attribute his lack of being arrested to the fact that he's made best friends with a law enforcement officer there in town?

A. No.

Q. That's just a coincidence that he stopped being arrested the last few years that he's lived in Tenaha?

A. He hasn't been arrested in a long time before — I mean, it doesn't matter.

Betsy denied an improper relationship between McClure and Walker, but she was clearly flustered at the end of her testimony.

No other witnesses testified during the detention hearing. Judge Giblin left the courtroom to deliberate on what he had heard. Within a short time, he came back to the courtroom. He began by acknowledging the support McClure had in the courtroom:

"To me that goes a lot for you, because I see your wife came up here, scared to death of testifying in court, she testified for you," he said. "You've got — it looks like you've got good community support out there and that goes a long way."

As Judge Giblin was speaking, McClure was beaming with confidence. It seemed he was certain the Judge wouldn't detain him and might just go ahead and throw the whole case out.

But a few moments later that confidence turned to disappointment when

Judge Giblin said, "And so what I have to do is, since I can't look into the future with a crystal ball, I have to look in the past to see whether or not you've done that for other Judges. That hurts you in this case. I'll be up front and tell you."

You could see the deflation in McClure's attitude instantly. Judge Giblin went on to explain that based on McClure's history of being revoked when he received probation on previous convictions, he couldn't reasonably conclude that McClure would not commit further crimes if released on bond. He ruled in favor of the Government and detained him pending trial.

McClure's trial for the felon in possession charge was scheduled for February 2012. He was placed in a federal holding facility in Livingston, Texas to await trial.

Giblin's ruling would be the subject of the first of many of self-written motions or appeals written by McClure that were based on obscure or misinterpreted legal arguments. As I would later find, McClure thought himself to be something of a legal scholar. While incarcerated at the Livingston facility, he had a law library available for research and he spent much of his time there searching for any possible way to attack the case against him by studying previous case law.

However, he also found time to talk to fellow inmates. One of them would later come forward.

13

I CAN'T GET YOU OUT OF SHIT RIGHT NOW

With McClure in jail, the next witness we sought to interview was Orlando Padron, the illegal immigrant from Mexico whose first name McClure had permanently tiled into the wall of his swimming pool.

According to Terrence Ford, Padron had once acted as a bodyguard for McClure on a drug deal he did with Kenneth McCaney. I was aware through recorded jail telephone conversations of McClure that Padron was staying at his home to protect McClure's wife, Betsy Smith, while McClure was in jail.

Blaine Gillis from the ATF joined Ranger Tom Davis and me in locating Padron. Gillis is an excellent investigator who speaks Spanish. It would come in handy more than once.

We found Padron living in a trailer house not far from McClure's home. He provided a Texas identification card which listed his address as 310 West Drive, the home of Rod McClure. Padron acknowledged he was living in the United States illegally and met McClure while working as a carpenter on McClure's new residence when it was being built in 2008 after his previous home was destroyed by fire.

Padron denied knowing of McClure being involved in any illegal activity. He appeared to be straightforward and didn't seem nervous.

But halfway through the interview he said, "I don't understand English very good."

Then Gillis began speaking to him in fluent Spanish he learned while working for the Immigration and Naturalization Service in San Antonio.

Padron's reaction was somewhat comical because it was obvious he wasn't expecting a corn-fed white boy to speak such good Spanish.

All we knew about him at that point was from Ford and it wasn't very detailed.

In hindsight, it was a bad tactical error that we didn't do a probable cause arrest of Padron that day, based on his admission of being in the United States illegally. I came to believe later that he probably would have had a lot to tell us.

Throughout McClure's incarceration, I obtained his recorded telephone conversations. All phone calls by inmates are routinely recorded. Because I received them in batches days or weeks after they took place, I didn't initially realize how much McClure was coordinating things on the outside.

Less than a week after being detained by Judge Giblin pending his trial on felon in possession, McClure told Padron he should be prepared to return to Mexico at a moment's notice. Below is a partial transcription of that phone call:

McClure: You remember I told you, you may have to go home, back to Mexico. You hear me?

Padron: Yeah.

McClure: Write me those phone numbers and addresses – the ones in Guadalajara.

Padron: Alrighty.

McClure: I need those phone numbers, I need your sister's phone number too amigo.

Padron: Okay

McClure: Alright then. Another thing, do not get in any trouble down there man, you understand?

Padron: I'm good cause I stopped drinking.

McClure: Alright cause I can't get you out of shit now, you hear me?

Padron: Yeah

McClure: And so don't be doing — don't do nothing stupid. Like I say, I can't get you out and it does no good for both of us to be up in here.

The day after we interviewed Padron, August 16, 2011, McClure found out from his wife, Betsy that Padron had been interviewed by us. He was livid she waited a day to tell him about it.

McClure, the autocrat, demanded to be informed immediately of such things, as it cost him valuable time in coordinating with Padron. I also learned from the jail calls that Betsty heard about our interview of Padron from Fred

Walker. This meant Padron had informed Walker about being contacted by us, and in turn, Walker passed the info along to her.

Another thing I learned from the jail calls was that McClure used a code name for Walker when he referred to him. He knew all his calls were being recorded but needed to get information from Walker about what was going on.

He and Walker didn't talk directly to each other — another indication to me they had something to hide — so when McClure and his wife referred to Walker, they used the code name "Old Boy" to describe him. It was almost funny because sometimes they forgot and said Walker's name anyway, and often it was very obvious from the context that they were referring to him.

The day McClure learned we had interviewed Orlando Padron, he ordered Padron to immediately return to Mexico. McClure thought we could use Padron to put pressure on him, and he wasn't taking any chances.

We never again saw Padron, although I learned from subsequent jail calls that he wanted to come back to Tenaha. If he did, we never found him.

—

We next contacted Sebastian Ewing, another individual Ford and McClure said was selling drugs stolen from the Marshal's Office. Not surprisingly, Ewing denied knowing anything about the illegal activity — although he was not as convincing in his denial as Padron had been.

The interview didn't last long, as Ewing wasn't much of a talker and he provided almost no details without being directly asked. He would resurface later in the case when a cooperating witness came forward who said he could buy marijuana and other drugs from him.

In late October 2011, an unexpected witness was discovered. I received a call from a woman who told me her husband, Bobby Roy Bachman[15], was currently incarcerated in a federal holding facility in Livingston, Texas awaiting sentencing on a drug case.

"My husband has a cellmate," she said. "I can't remember his name but he told Bobby he broke into a police evidence room and stole all the drugs."

If true, Bachman could be a compelling witness against McClure.

I checked his criminal history and background and learned he was not from anywhere near Tenaha. This meant he most likely didn't previously know McClure, nor have any familiarity with the case.

---

[15] Not his real name.

A cellmate's testimony can be very incriminating against a defendant. However, their credibility can be reasonably attacked as they likely have lengthy criminal histories and may be motivated to lie to help themselves get a reduction of sentence. Independent corroboration of their statement is therefore very important.

Prosecutor Lisa Flournoy, Ranger Tom Davis, ATF Agent Blaine Gillis and I traveled to Livingston to meet with Bobby Roy Bachman. He was facing a very lengthy sentence for a drug related conviction. He was up front with us, and said that he would like to get whatever reduction he could. But he asked for no promises nor did he seem to hold anything back.

"I've had several conversations with this guy McClure that started shortly after he got here," he said. "McClure told me he had a cousin in law enforcement who helped him steal $2 to $4 million worth of cocaine, other drugs, guns and a bulletproof vest from a police evidence locker. He told me the Feds were using information against him from a friend of his who was jammed up on other charges."

He continued, without needing any encouragement.

"McClure told me there had been a search warrant at his house and they were looking for video surveillance recordings and saw a gun nearby where McClure was sitting," Bachman said.

His information certainly was credible. Other than McClure greatly inflating the value of the drugs — probably to build himself up to Bachman — the story was consistent with what we already knew. And it was coming from a person whose only source of the information would most likely have been McClure himself.

14

WHAT ABOUT FRED?

To seal the case against McClure, the only work left to be completed was to get Kenneth McCaney — the Shreveport, Louisiana connection — to cooperate. The case against Fred Walker, the law enforcement officer who was the main subject of the case, however, was only circumstantial and largely based on hearsay.

For example, McClure sent text messages with accompanying photographs listing and showing the various drugs that had been stolen from the Marshal's Office evidence room to Terrence Ford. We could directly connect McClure's cell phone number to the texts and photos.

In addition, he had numerous conversations with Ford in which he detailed the entire illegal scheme. That meant we could use the text messages, the photos, and Ford's testimony of McClure's involvement.

We had McClure's girlfriend, Amy Johnson, who could testify to writing the Zetas letter at his request. Bobby Roy Bachman could testify to McClure's jailhouse admission. All of this made a compelling case against McClure.

Unfortunately, we found no such evidence directly linking Walker to the scheme. Ford's and Bachman's statements referring to Walker were hearsay from McClure, which is not admissible in court. The only direct statement linking Walker to anything illegal would be testimony from McClure himself, and he wasn't showing any signs of cooperating.

So at this point in the case, prosecutor Lisa Flournoy made the decision to continue the drug trafficking/public corruption case, shifting the focus to finding evidence directly incriminating Fred Walker, and separately adjudicate the felon in possession matter against McClure.

She reasoned that the case was a sideline issue that had been thrown up by McClure to deflect from the ongoing case, and should be fairly easy to get out of the way.

In addition, motivation to get a reduced sentence might spur McClure to reconsider cooperating against Walker. If we found direct evidence against Walker for drug trafficking, he would be indicted along with McClure.

The rationale made sense. But this was the last time I would make the assumption that anything involving Rod McClure would be rational.

For no particular reason other than administrative simplicity, I did not open a separate case file relating to the illegal wiretapping allegations made by McClure. Nor did I open a separate case file relating to the felon in possession case which inadvertently sprung from the wiretapping search warrant at McClure's home.

There is no administrative policy in the FBI requiring Agents to open separate case files for every type of violation committed in a particular investigation. But this was something else McClure would later try to exploit, arguing to have the case thrown out on a technicality.

To begin directly linking Fred Walker to the burglary, I reviewed what we knew up to this point — and what we might have overlooked.

I obtained the Sheriff's Office dispatch records for the night of the burglary. Because it was such a small agency, the Tenaha City Marshal's Office used the Shelby County Sheriff's Office dispatchers for calls and complaints.

Around 10 p.m. on August 21, the night before Walker reported finding the Marshal's Office burglary, he was dispatched to a home just outside of the city limits about a complaint of people riding noisy four-wheelers.

The dispatch logs revealed Walker responded back that he had checked it out and found nothing. Gillis and I went to the home from where the complaint call originated. No one was home when we came by so I left a business card and a note asking them to call back.

I subsequently received a call from a woman who recalled, "I remember calling the Sheriff's Office about some noisy four-wheelers but nobody from law enforcement came by the house to respond."

Now this didn't mean Walker didn't respond to the call, but it showed he didn't bother to follow up with the complainant.

We also learned there had been a private party in a large meeting room that doubled as a reception hall within the same building as the Marshal's Office and only separated by one locked door. The party ended sometime before 10:30 p.m.

When he first reported finding the burglary, Walker told District Attorney Investigator Kevin Windham he had driven by the office the night before at approximately 10:30 and saw no one there. Walker told Windham he went into the office and worked on a file until going home around midnight. He returned at 6:50 a.m., the next morning, August 22, and found the burglary.

After the simultaneous interviews of Ford, Walker and McClure on August 8, 2011, I began receiving periodic calls from Carolyn Walsh[16], the ex-wife of Fred Walker.

Carolyn was divorced from Walker but continued living in the same house with him until just after this case broke open. I learned from recorded jail conversations that Rod McClure mistakenly believed Carolyn Walsh was the informant behind all the troubles he was experiencing. As a result, Fred kicked her out of the house following McClure's arrest.

I asked her about Walker's whereabouts the night of the burglary and the day it was discovered. Carolyn recalled Walker being home the night the burglary occurred but acknowledged she went to bed early and would not have necessarily awakened if he had left during the night.

We couldn't be sure if Walker left the house because of the four-wheelers complaint, but if he did, Carolyn didn't remember it. She specifically recalled however Walker leaving early the next morning, which would have been a Sunday.

Carolyn said this was highly unusual in two ways: "Fred is basically lazy, so he never went into the office that early and he rarely worked on Sundays."

"I do recall him leaving early that Sunday morning though," she said. "I remember it because it was so unusual. So I called him to find out what was going on. He didn't say why he had left early but told me the Marshal's Office had been burglarized. He also told me about finding a Spanish language letter and it looked like a Mexican gang had done it."

We located a witness named Becky Sayles[17] who worked as a clerk at a 24-hour convenience store down the street from the Marshal's Office.

Sayles recalled seeing Walker loading a box into his patrol car in front of the Marshal's Office sometime between the hours of 1 a.m. and 2 a.m. on August 22. Sayles' information was good, but conflicted with Carolyn Walsh's

---

[16] Not her real name.

[17] Not her real name.

recollection of Walker being at home.

Carolyn told us during the time period when the Marshal's Office burglary happened, she did notice Fred had a lot of cash. We already knew this from our financial analysis that he was making unexplained cash deposits.

In addition to the dispatch logs and financial records, I also analyzed Fred Walker's telephone calls in great detail. It again struck me how many calls were made daily between him and McClure — sometimes as many as 30 calls, but averaging about 15 per day. And the times of the calls ranged throughout the day and night.

In the time period I analyzed, approximately one year prior to the burglary, I found there were over 2,600 calls between Walker and McClure.

In addition, Walker made an equal number of calls to his secretary Marilyn Andrews and a friend of hers named Sherry Stevens.[18] In later interviews of Andrews and Stevens, they acknowledged the large number of calls and said Walker liked to gossip.

Despite some suspicious findings, we could find nothing directly linking Walker to the burglary like we had against McClure. It was purely a circumstantial case and would be a toss-up if we took it to trial.

---

[18] Not her real name.

15

MCCLURE'S DAY IN COURT

In the beginning months of 2012, as we continued the investigation in hopes of finding direct evidence against Fred Walker, McClure's felon in possession of a firearm case was nearing its February trial date.

It was to be held in the United States District Court of Judge Ron Clark in Beaumont. I received a call from federal prosecutor Lisa Flournoy about a notice she received from the court advising that McClure had filed a motion seeking an evidence suppression hearing.

Even though the deadline for such motions had passed, Judge Clark allowed the motion and set a hearing for February 7.

In the months since McClure's detention hearing the previous August, he replaced John McElroy, his appointed attorney from the United States Public Defender's Office, because as I learned from his jail calls, he felt McElroy would simply plead his case out and not put any effort into fighting it.

McClure speculated he could not beat the case at trial since it was pretty clear cut: He was a felon and had been found in possession of 13 guns at his home. He might, however, have a chance to have the evidence against him — namely the 13 guns — suppressed or excluded from the case if he could prove the search warrant that brought us to his home was invalid.

This is a theory commonly known in law as Fruit of the Poisonous Tree. It means if the source of evidence, the tree (or in this case the search warrant allowing us into his home) is tainted, then any fruits of that tree — the 13 guns — is also tainted and cannot be used as evidence.

Since McClure did not trust McElroy to be his attorney, he coordinated with his father to hire an outside attorney. He had very little concern for how much it would cost, because he intended for Fred Walker to pay for it.

Over several recorded jail conversations, McClure was emphatic that Old Boy, his code word for Walker, would pay for the attorney because of what McClure knew about him. In a conversation he had with someone named Tweetie, McClure said:

"Old Boy Fred, uh, it's like this right here — he gonna come up with some money from his sugar mama and everything, take care of my wife and kids…It's like this right here, gonna take care of Betsy and them, he gonna come up with some more cash for them and everything — or his fat ass be up in here. Do you understand me?

The "sugar mama" McClure was referring to was Walker's former secretary, Marilyn Andrews, who was well off by small town Texas standards. Unfortunately, though, he never spelled out specifically what he knew that would put Walker in jail.

McClure was equally emphatic however that he wanted a lawyer that would do what he told them to do. There was no longer any hint about cooperating. Now he was going to fight the case as hard as he could.

I believe this newfound resolve to fight was based on what he learned from the discovery documents turned over to him in preparation for trial.

In a criminal case, the prosecution is required to turn over investigative documents and to reveal evidence against a defendant prior to trial, to allow the attorney to prepare a defense against the charges.

Through discovery, McClure became aware of Terrence Ford's cooperation and some of the extent of what we knew. He probably made a calculated decision that if he were found guilty in a subsequent case relating to the drug trafficking from the Marshal's Office evidence room, he would be facing significant prison time, even if he pleaded guilty and received a lesser sentence. It would therefore make sense to try to get everything he knew we had at that point thrown out.

We would later learn from Agents and Task Force Officers at the DEA who handled McClure when he was an informant for them in the 1990s that he was eager in providing information about others dealing drugs. They came to suspect that McClure was dealing drugs and was using his status as an informant to eliminate competitors by making cases on them.

"McClure would inform on his own mother if it got him out of trouble," one of his handlers told me.

In fact, in 2011, when we first arrived at his home to execute the search warrant, McClure threw out names of DEA Agents he had worked with as way of trying to convince us he was an okay guy.

So if he had been such an eager informant, why not inform on Fred Walker about the stolen evidentiary drugs? Most every criminal involved in corrupt relationships with law enforcement officers knows they have an ace up their sleeve if they get caught on other charges — because of the high priority of catching corrupt officers.

McClure was well aware, through his previous interviews with us, that Fred Walker was the real target of our case and we wanted McClure's cooperation. Why was he now so adamant about fighting?

At that point in the case, the government would likely have dismissed the gun case altogether and negotiated a very light sentence for drug trafficking, possibly probation, in return for truthful information about a dirty cop.

I eventually formed the opinion that his reason for not cooperating was tied to the death of David Thompson. Thompson might have indeed committed suicide — or something more sinister may have happened.

I will detail the suspicious aspects of Thompson's death later, but it was around this time that I developed the opinion that McClure and Walker were protecting each other from something more serious than stealing drugs from an evidence room.

This need to have the case thrown out entirely meant McClure needed an attorney who would take the matter to trial if need be, even in the face of overwhelming evidence, and be willing to argue the most technical and frivolous points. In a recorded jail conversation, McClure told his father that he needed an attorney who would do what he told him to do and if need be he (McClure) would file the needed motions "my own motherfucking self".

McClure found the attorney he was looking for in Lori Mack, a Houston based attorney who was just coming off a suspension from the Texas Bar Association for failing to keep a client informed about their case. Mack had never defended a case in federal court and was eager to get the work. As the case moved forward, I felt Mack was in way over her head, that she told McClure what he wanted to hear, and was unprepared to deal with his controlling personality.

True to his word, McClure himself wrote the motion seeking the suppression hearing. Mack simply adopted his work and filed it with the court under her own name.

In a letter he later mailed to Judge Ron Clark complaining about Mack, McClure said "she took a Suppression Motion that I had written *pro se*[19] and

---

[19] Pro Se is a latin phrase meaning "on one's own behalf."

given to my father in September and filed it with(out) discussing it with me."

It turned out to be one of many motions McClure would file in various federal courts.

In several jail conversations with his wife and his father, McClure discussed the ways he planned to attack the search warrant and more specifically, the affidavit which accompanied it. The affidavit is a statement of facts laying out the probable cause a judge relies on to issue a search warrant.

Probable cause, the standard required for a search and arrest warrants, exists if the facts and circumstances would cause a reasonable person to conclude that a crime has been committed. A search warrant affidavit must include specific facts of a particular case to establish that a crime has been committed, and a particular description of the place to be searched.

—

By some quirk of small town street numbering, McClure's home address was listed on the county tax rolls as 410 West Drive — even though his home prominently displayed 310 as its address and McClure's driver's license also showed 310 West Drive.

This is what McClure's attorney at the detention hearing was questioning me about. McClure planned to use this discrepancy to argue the search warrant was illegal under the constitutional requirement that the place to be searched must be particularly described.

In addition to the address discrepancy, McClure's motion also employed a shotgun approach of arguments. That is he threw in practically every possible argument in law trying to render the search warrant illegal. A common way this is referred to is: "Throw some shit against a wall and see how much will stick."

It didn't seem to matter to him that practically every point he raised could be easily refuted. McClure's motion seeking the suppression hearing was actually very well written. He had clearly put in a lot of thought and effort. In listing some of his grievances, McClure said the following:

"The actions of the Government violated the Defendant's rights in that:

The warrant is insufficient on its face;

The items seized are not the items described in the warrant;

There was no probable cause for believing the existence of the grounds on which the warrant was issued;

The warrant was illegally executed;

The search and seizure was conducted in bad faith."

Among his arguments was that any admissions he made were "elicited through illegal police interrogation after the Defendant had requested the assistance of counsel." McClure included both the confession at his home during the search warrant and the broader confession made during his transport to Beaumont. He asked they be thrown out, even though these confessions had nothing to do with the case at hand — charges of being a felon in possession of a firearm.

McClure inadvertently wrote an ironic statement in his suppression motion regarding credibility. In the search warrant affidavit, I included a brief statement about information given to me by Carolyn Walsh, Fred Walker's ex-wife, who was still living with him at the time. McClure emphatically but wrongly believed that Carolyn had turned over a stolen computer to me.

To show the affidavit contained false information, McClure wrote "Witness Carolyn Walsh is a convicted felon, which calls into question her credibility."

Under the same reasoning then, couldn't the credibility of McClure's entire motion be called into question since he also was a convicted felon? I'm certain though the irony never occurred to him.

In most circumstances, an evidence suppression hearing is essentially a trial. The rules are not as formal and there is no jury, but if key evidence to be used by the prosecution is suppressed, the government's case can be greatly weakened.

On the other hand, if the defendant fails to have evidence against him suppressed, he will likely lose at trial if the evidence is persuasive of his guilt. In McClure's hearing, it was all or nothing.

McClure, Texas Ranger Tom Davis and I all testified at the suppression hearing. Prosecutor Lisa Flournoy called me to the stand first. As previously mentioned, because McClure's motion to suppress went far beyond simply attempting to exclude evidence in the case at hand — felon in possession of a firearm — Lisa began her questioning of me with the entire background of our work in Tenaha.

Although McClure was claiming his address was 410 West Drive in an effort to invalidate the search warrant, we were able to show he never used that address. In addition to the number "310" clearly displayed on the house we searched, Lisa brought out several instances where he used "310" as shown by the following line of her questioning of me:

Q: I now show you what's been marked as Government's Exhibit C. And what is that?

A: That is a printout of Mr. McClure's driver's license information.

Q: Okay. And on the first line under Mr. McClure's picture, what is the address listed for Mr. McClure's residence?

A: 310 West Drive, Tenaha, Texas.

Lisa then focused on how we developed the probable cause for the search warrant — McClure himself admitting he possessed secretly recorded conversations in his home in a voluntary and non-custodial interview:

Q: Did he (McClure) provide any information about where any evidence might be regarding the recordings that were made of the mayor and Barry Washington?

A: He did. He provided a specific indication of where the recording devices had been placed as well as where some recordings presently were located.

Q: And where did he state they were?

A: He indicated that they were in his house, and made a slight motion pointing to his home.

Q: Where is Mr. McClure's home in relation to his computer business?

A: It sits immediately adjacent to it.

Q: About what distance would you say there is between the Computer Clinic and Mr. McClure's home?

A: I would say 40 feet.

Along with other testimony, this line of questioning established our probable cause — the legal justification for searching McClure's home. Lisa then began questioning me about finding guns in the home during the search:

Q: Let me just ask you this — Was the search warrant affidavit that was presented to the Court to search Mr. McClure's home for evidence of the interception of communications just a ruse to get into Mr. McClure's home so you could hopefully find firearms?

A: No, it was not.

Q: Were you legitimately investigating and searching for evidence related to a federal crime, non-firearm related?

A: Yes I was.

Q: And had you had an opportunity to look at Mr. McClure's criminal history prior to the search warrant?

A: I had.

Q: And were you aware whether or not Mr. McClure had a prior felony conviction?

A: I was aware of that, yes.

Q: Were you aware that it was illegal under federal law for Mr. McClure to possess firearms when you executed the search warrant?

A: I was.

Q: Did you see firearms that were located within a gun cabinet located at the McClure residence?

A: I did see them, yes.

Q: Were all of these firearms accessible to Mr. McClure at the residence?

A: Yes.

After my direct testimony, McClure's attorney, Lori Mack, conducted her cross examination of me. She began by asking several questions regarding the Jack Frost extortion letters and my interview of Terrence Ford.

Mack then switched gears and asked several questions about the execution of the search warrant. She started off, I think, with the intention of trying to establish one of the arguments McClure had alleged in his motion. She wanted to convince the judge that we had used heavy-handed tactics when "the Defendant answered the door to numerous Agents with weapons drawn and brandished at him."

Q: When you arrived at the defendant's home, did you knock on the door personally?

A: I don't recall if I did. I was at the front door, but I don't recall if I'm the one that actually knocked or not.

Q: Okay. And what happened after that?

A: Well there was a knock at the door, an announcement of "Police — search warrant." Mr. McClure opened the door. He was brought out of the house, and that's where it started.

Q: Okay. Were guns drawn?

A: Yes.

Q: How many Agents had their guns drawn, approximately?

A: I don't know.

Q: More than 10? Less than five?

A: I don't know. I didn't necessarily pay attention to other Agents. I had my own gun drawn.

The tone of her voice, her phrasing and the stress on certain words in her questioning were accusatory. This is a tactic many defense attorneys use when questioning prosecution witnesses to subconsciously influence a jury — or in this case a judge — that the witness is hiding something, lying or has done something wrong.

For example, by using a normal tone of voice with no stress on any particular word, the question "Did you eat a cheeseburger at lunch?" is innocuous. However, if I change to an accusatory tone of voice, change the phrasing and stress certain words, the same question can be asked "ISN'T it true that YOU ate a CHEESEBURGER at LUNCH, sir?!"

The way to counter such tactics is to answer with a calm and steady tone and not take the bait and become defensive, angry or combative.

Mack was trying to communicate that we had been overly intimidating and heavy-handed towards McClure and show the judge he was a helpless victim being picked on by the government.

Mack's questioning continued:

Q: Okay. All right. And you testified earlier as to why you felt this was necessary?

A: Any search warrant, I'm going to have my gun drawn, ma'am.

Q: Okay. Is that standard operating procedure?

A: Yes ma'am.

Q: Okay. When Mr. McClure answered the door, was he threatening in any way?

A: No.

Q: Did he have a gun on him?

A: No.

The technical answer to that question was no; but he did have 13 guns inside the house.

Although my answer to the question of having my gun drawn was technically incorrect in that there is no specific requirement that I know of in the FBI that requires an Agent to have their gun drawn — it is something that is left to the discretion of each Agent — it was my personal standard operating procedure.

Certainly, conducting a search warrant at the home of a felon whose criminal history included shooting at and wounding his own cousin and who we believed might be in possession of several guns, a ballistic vest and a hand grenade, it wasn't imprudent to have my gun drawn.

In a subsequent question, still covering the search warrant, Mack may not have agreed with my answer at the time, but I bet she later came to understand and strongly agree with it:

Q: What did you question him about or say to him?

A: Well, to be very honest, it was very difficult to contain Mr. McClure. He was very talkative.

Because the suppression motion — filed by Mack but written by McClure — contained every facet of the investigation, Lisa Flournoy called Texas Ranger Tom Davis to testify regarding the confession McClure initiated during the two-hour drive from Lufkin to Beaumont for his initial appearance.

McClure was claiming that "any statements allegedly attributed to the Defendant were made as a result of illegal custodial interrogation, without proper warning under Miranda."

In retrospect, Lisa probably should have simply argued to Judge Clark that McClure's car ride confession was not pertinent to McClure being a felon in possession of a firearm but part of a separate investigation. But her strategy was to simply address all the arguments McClure's motion brought up. Lisa's questioning of Ranger Davis continued:

Q: So, on the way down there (Beaumont), Mr. McClure — does he begin talking to you and Agent Lane?

A: He told us he wanted to talk to us; so, while we were still in the parking lot of the drugstore,[20] I read him his Miranda warning again and explained to him and asked him if he was sure he wanted to talk to us since the previous two days he had told us he did not want to talk to us. He assured

---

[20] Ranger Davis and Agent Lane had stopped at a drugstore at McClure's request for baby aspirin, which he said was part of a treatment program stemming from a previous stroke he suffered.

us he did, and he began to talk to us.

Q: And the Miranda that you read him, was that read from a card that you carry on your person?

A: It's a card that I carry in my notebook.

Q: And did Mr. McClure sign that card to indicate that he had, in fact waived his rights?

A: No. Mr. McClure was handcuffed and not able to make a signature.

Q: Do you feel confident at that time that he had been advised and was still willing to talk to you and Agent Lane?

A: Yes ma'am. He was adamant about talking to us. We had to slow him down and stop him several times because he wanted to talk to us so badly. We had to stop him in order to get the Miranda in and explain to him that, you know, he had a right not to talk to us; and yet he continued.

Mack conducted no cross-examination of Ranger Davis, and Lisa Flournoy told the Court she had no further witnesses. Mack then called McClure to the stand for his direct examination.

He displayed an arrogant confidence as he took the stand and seemed certain Judge Clark was in awe of the suppression motion he had written.

Since he was so confident the entire search warrant would be thrown out based on the address discrepancy of 410 West Drive vs. 310 West Drive, he seemed barely able to contain himself as he answered the question:

Q: Where do you live?

A: 410 West Drive, Tenaha, Texas.

As he answered McClure had a slight smirk and greatly stressed the word "four." To explain why the home itself had the address 310 clearly marked on it by a decorative plaque, Mack asked:

Q: Next to the front door is a sign. What does that sign say?

A: 310

Q: Mr. McClure you testified that your address is 410 West Drive. Why is there a sign that says "310"?

A: Because that address was taken off of my computer shop, which is 310, and placed on the house in '08. During '08, like I said, our home had burned down and we were staying in a camper trailer on the property right behind my computer shop and so, we were living in the computer shop. Well, we needed power for the construction crew to build the home; and the light company would not give us a temporary because there was no address with some numbers on the thing.

Q: So you're testifying that sign actually came from another building on the property?

A: It came off my computer shop. Yes ma'am…My computer shop is 310 West Drive.

McClure was testifying that a very nice, decorative brass address plaque had been attached to a rundown, tiny building — a shed, essentially. The only indication it was a business was an amateurish hand-painted sign and a faded handwritten note in a window saying deliveries should be left at the main house. I didn't buy it for a minute.

After the hearing, I went back and checked several records I had gathered during the investigation — one of which was the Texas Department of Public Safety Public Sex Offender Registry. McClure had to register as a Sex Offender after a conviction on Attempted Sexual Assault. On the DPS registry, McClure listed both his address and his employment as 310 West Drive. Since he was now testifying that his residence was 410, he was either lying now or had been lying to the DPS.

I found another record through City Marshal Tom Reader. Reader had taken over Fred Walker's position after Walker resigned to become Constable. Reader found a Tenaha Volunteer Fire Department Response Report relating to the fire McClure described that burned his previous home down in late 2007. What address had been given for the home that burned down? 310 West Drive. That was in direct contradiction to his testimony that day in the suppression hearing:

Q: What (house) was there before?

A: We had a frame home that had caught fire and had burned down

Q: So the previous house on that property at 410 was burned down?

A: Yes ma'am.

I knew McClure was willing to say anything, when during his testimony regarding our interview of him during the execution of the search warrant he said

A: After they cleared the home and everything, they took me back into the house and, with the handcuffs on, they set me down at my breakfast nook.

Q: So you were handcuffed at the time you were sat down?

A: Oh yes ma'am.

Q: Were you given any sort of Miranda warnings?

A: No ma'am.

Q: Were the cuffs ever taken off you?

A: No ma'am.

It was at that moment I decided to myself if I ever had occasion to talk with McClure again it would be recorded or I wouldn't talk with him at all. Although the FBI didn't routinely record interviews, it was allowed if circumstances justified it.

Also, if McClure ever had the intention of cooperating and testifying against Walker, he had severely damaged his credibility with us because he had been read his Miranda warning and had not been handcuffed during the interview. How could we let him testify to anything, knowing he wasn't being truthful about this?

During the hearing, there did appear to be some tension between McClure and his attorney, Lori Mack. I would later find from jail recordings that McClure desperately wanted Fred Walker to testify that the Dell laptop from which we obtained the photos of him shouldering a rifle had been stolen.

Mack questioned me about the laptop but had nowhere to go when I told her it had been properly received by City Marshal Tom Reader from Fred Walker because it was city property and that Reader had then turned it over to me.

———

McClure's vision of making legal history that day was shattered by Judge Ron Clark, who in a very detailed and reasoned judgment, ruled against him on every point.

He found McClure's argument about the address to be non-persuasive and legally of no importance because the home had been accurately described otherwise in the affidavit, including the 310 address plaque permanently attached to the house. In other words, there was no doubt about what house we intended to search and had accurately executed the warrant at the home described in the affidavit.

Judge Clark painstakingly went over all the other arguments McClure made and ruled against him on all of them. He found the search warrant to be valid in all respects and therefore allowed the 13 guns found during the search could be used as evidence against McClure for being a felon in possession of a firearm.

Regarding McClure's admissions about the drug trafficking and claims he was forced to make them under duress, Judge Clark ruled they were not relevant to the case with which he was charged and excluded them from being used.

McClure took this as a victory — but he failed to realize prosecutor Lisa Flournoy didn't plan to use these admissions of drug trafficking in the gun possession case anyway. Judge Clark only addressed them because McClure had included them in his broad motion seeking the suppression hearing.

Judge Clark did scold the government (i.e. me) for not recording the statements from McClure. I fully agreed and took the lesson to heart. Indeed, I would ensure all future interactions with McClure would be recorded.

Having lost at the suppression hearing, McClure was told by Mack that the only option was to plead guilty. I learned this from recorded jail conversations he had with family members.

It was apparent in his subsequent jail calls that McClure, who had been so confident his suppression motion would win the day and he would be able to go home, was heartbroken the judge had overwhelmingly failed to see the brilliance of his arguments.

—

On February 14, 2012, McClure pleaded guilty to one count of felon in possession of a firearm. The hearing was held before Judge Clark, who went through the procedure in a very methodical and thorough fashion.

He started out by asking if McClure had ever been treated for mental illness and if he was currently under any sort of mental impairment. McClure answered no to both questions. Judge Clark questioned him about his satisfaction with the performance of his attorney, Lori Mack — whether he had fully discussed the facts of the case with her about possible witnesses, or evidence that might be produced showing his innocence. McClure testified he was fully satisfied with Mack's representation.

Judge Clark went into detail, noting that McClure would be giving up his right to a trial. At times, it almost seemed the judge was trying to talk McClure out of pleading guilty.

Finally, he explained that by pleading guilty, McClure would also be giving up his right to appeal the case — except under the exceptions of ineffective assistance of counsel and sentence in excess of statutory maximum.

Judge Clark explained that since McClure had already testified he was satisfied with his counsel, it would make it very difficult for him to later appeal ineffective assistance.

Regarding the second exception, Judge Clark told McClure the chance of him (Clark) making a mistake at sentencing was very slim. McClure agreed and Judge Clark found him guilty based on the guilty plea. Sentencing was set for July pending the results of a pre-sentence investigation by the United States Probation Office.

From our point of view, the annoyance of the felon in possession issue, which I believed from the beginning was a red herring thrown out by McClure, was over and now we could get back to focusing on the drug trafficking investigation. Our aim from this point on would be finding incriminating direct evidence against Fred Walker to go along with the circumstantial evidence we already had.

Since it was clear we couldn't count on McClure to cooperate, we would have to find it without his help.

I subsequently learned from jail conversations that McClure would have been surprised to know we were continuing the investigation, because he had formed the opinion that by pleading guilty, all his troubles, not just the felon in possession case but the more significant drug trafficking case, had been washed away by his guilty plea.

This mistaken conclusion on his part would be the subject of a later legal attack that he used over and over, attempting to get the case thrown out.

16

I AM CAIN

Not long after McClure pleaded guilty to felon in possession, Texas Ranger Tom Davis took a promotion, which moved him from investigative work to management and administrative duties. Blaine Gillis from the ATF and I continued working together and we kept Davis in the loop as the investigation continued. If the case went to trial, Davis would likely have to testify regarding McClure's confession made during the transport to Beaumont.

We located Kenneth "Cain" McCaney and set up an interview with him through the attorney representing him on the Louisiana drug charge. Surprisingly, the attorney allowed McCaney to meet with us without him being present. The interview started with McCaney acknowledging he knew McClure.

"Yeah I know him, my wife and his wife went to high school together," he said. "He's a computer guy and he did some work on my computer. I know he got in trouble last year."

McCaney also acknowledged meeting McClure once at a Shreveport casino, and McClure was accompanied by a woman who was not his wife. From his description of the woman, we concluded he was talking about Amy Johnson, McClure's girlfriend who wrote the phony Zetas letter left at the Marshal's Office burglary scene.

When the questioning came around to whether McCaney had knowledge or involvement with McClure in drug trafficking, he admitted seeing McClure use cocaine in his computer shop. Otherwise, McCaney became very reluctant and like Terrence Ford, indicated he knew some things that could incriminate himself.

As with Ford, we told McCaney we would have to consult with the United States Attorney's Office and prosecutor Lisa Flournoy before we could go any further.

After a discussion with Flournoy, it was decided to offer McCaney a proffer session to learn what he knew. A subsequent interview with him was set up and this time, he was accompanied by his attorney.

McCaney said he had been introduced to McClure at some point in early spring or summer 2010 at a Shreveport nightclub named The Warehouse. McCaney, who acknowledged he had previously dealt drugs, said his conversation with McClure started off with small talk but quickly turned to the subject of dealing drugs.

"Rod said he was looking for someone to help him sell drugs in Shreveport and he knew a cop that would provide protection from getting arrested," McCaney said.

"Did he give you the name of the cop he was talking about?" I asked.

"No he never mentioned the name," he responded.

He described his first drug deal with McClure. The two met in Logansport, Louisiana, a small town 15 miles from Tenaha, sitting on the east bank of the Sabine River, which separates Texas and Louisiana. McCaney said McClure fronted him approximately 10 pounds of marijuana. Over the next three days, McCaney sold the marijuana in the Shreveport area for $5,500. He gave McClure $3,500 and kept $2,000 for himself.

McCaney said when they met back in Logansport so he could give McClure the money, McClure told him there were only certain times of the day when McCaney could travel to Tenaha when the cop he mentioned during their first meeting could protect him.

Blaine Gillis and I both surmised McClure was talking about the need to avoid conducting drug deals when Deputy City Marshal Barry Washington was on duty in Tenaha.

But again, McCaney said McClure didn't use any specific names.

By this point in the investigation, we suspected it was likely the illegal wiretapping Walker and McClure set up in Washington's office was not meant to gain intelligence about the *Morrow* federal civil case so Walker could "cover his ass," as McClure previously told us.

It was more likely conducted with the intention of catching Washington in a compromising position, so he could be forced to resign from the Marshal's

Office. This would remove the threat of their drug trafficking operation being discovered by Washington.

About two weeks after their first deal together, McCaney said he traveled to Tenaha to meet McClure for another deal. They met at a truck stop on Highway 59. This time though McClure added a little cloak-and-dagger to the situation.

"Rod had me get into his Hummer and told me to close my eyes and keep them covered with my hands. He said he didn't fully trust me."

McCaney said they drove a short period.

"We crossed over a railroad track and drove briefly on a bumpy road," he recounted. "When we stopped, Rod said I could look. We were in a rundown looking trailer park."

The trailer they visited appeared to be lived-in, but McCaney said no one else was present and he didn't see any other cars.

"We went inside this one trailer and I saw several pounds of marijuana wrapped in plastic," McCaney said. "I took about 20 pounds of what I considered to be the best. I could tell some of the weed wasn't very good quality."

Afterwards he and McClure got back in the Hummer and McCaney again covered his eyes and they returned to the truck stop. McCaney was able to sell the marijuana for $11,000. He gave McClure $7,000 and kept the remaining $4,000 for himself.

About two weeks after the second marijuana deal, McCaney and McClure figured out that their wives had gone to high school together.

"Once we figured out that our wives knew each other, Rod started trusting me and we all started seeing each other socially," he said.

This contradicted McClure's claim about not knowing "Cain's" real name but it was clear why he didn't want us to find him — McCaney would be a very damaging witness against him.

McCaney said a third deal was set up. This time, McCaney went to McClure's computer shop and obtained about 50 pounds of marijuana. McCaney recalled making about $25,000 from this deal, keeping around $7,000 for himself.

McCaney said that not long after the third marijuana deal, "Rod became paranoid that people were after him. He said he got a letter from a DA wanting $250,000 and threatening to burn his world down. After he got that letter, Rod started wearing a bulletproof vest everywhere he went."

McCaney became nervous about dealing with McClure at this point, he said. He gradually lost contact with him, and they did no further drug deals together.

I checked cell phone records and confirmed they were in contact throughout the spring and summer of 2010. The telephonic contact slowed in the fall and stopped not long after McClure would have received the Jack Frost extortion letter from Terrence Ford.

After McCaney's proffer, Blaine Gillis and I met him in Logansport and had him ride with us for the short distance to Tenaha. We started at the convenience store where McCaney had met McClure prior to the second drug deal.

According to his account, McCaney and McClure had driven over some railroad tracks. As the railroad tracks were almost directly across the street from the convenience store, we crossed them and drove to the areas of town where there were trailer homes. Our search didn't take that long.

"There it is," McCaney said. "That's it, for sure."

He pointed out an old brown trailer house on Waller Creek Drive. Gillis and I were later able to interview the owner of the trailer. It had been rented to Orlando Padron at the time when McCaney went there with McClure to pick up the 20 pounds of marijuana.

In addition to connecting a trailer home to Padron — McClure's almost-adopted son who fled back to Mexico at his orders — there was another suspicious aspect regarding the location of the trailer.

It was located on Waller Creek Drive — the same street on which David Thompson lived. Because Waller Creek turned sharply after Thompson's home and circled back, Padron's trailer was situated less than 400 yards through some woods. It would mean someone could visit Thompson's home by parking at Padron's trailer and walking through the woods — making it very unlikely anyone would be seen going to the house. Had someone taken advantage of this to stage a suicide at Thompson's home?

With McCaney's proffer, we now had McClure solidly implicated in drug trafficking and the staged Marshal's Office burglary with a second witness independent from Terrence Ford. Even without the two confessions McClure previously made, and which he was likely to recant, we felt strongly we could prove the case against him.

But we were still left with only a circumstantial case against Fred Walker. The only direct evidence of Walker's involvement was McClure's confession, which we could not count on. McClure's sentencing for his guilty plea was set for July 31. Prosecutor Lisa Flournoy said she would consider whether or not to include Walker in the drug trafficking indictment with McClure after the felon in possession sentencing. The reasoning was once he was sentenced on the felon in possession case, he might decide to cooperate.

Flournoy told McClure's attorney, Lori Mack, that a larger and more significant case was coming against him after the felon in possession case, and the government wanted his cooperation. Mack never responded.

—

When McClure was sentenced on the felon in possession case, Judge Ron Clark allowed him to make a statement. McClure, reading from prepared notes, made his introduction:

"Judge Clark, it's been said that a picture tells a story in a thousand words. The words I recite to the court today are my colors, these papers I read from are my canvas, and my ink pen is my brush. I paint, your honor, to complete an incomplete picture of myself presented to you in the PSR (Pre-Sentence Report). The picture I unveil, your Honor is only 39 percent complete since I am only 39 years old."

He went on to describe his checkered past and mistakes he made. Throughout his statement, he quoted from poet John Keats, John Adams, George Washington, The Bible, poet John Milton, Thomas Edison, and the Apostle Paul.

He cited Webster's dictionary in defining "responsibility" as "liable to be called on to answer for one's conduct." He read his statement in a humble and reserved tone. He acknowledged possessing the guns and he said he took responsibility for them being in his home. Then he excused his behavior by saying:

"I just don't know how I misread the Texas Penal Code 46.04. When the officers came through my door, it was the first thing I quoted to them. I said 'Texas law says I could have it.' I know it has no bearing, your Honor; but I had talked to state troopers. I even talked to a state representative, Wayne Christian; and everyone told me I was fine. I had no idea that federal law was ever going to come into play with anything that I was doing."

In imposing McClure's sentence, Judge Clark pointed out McClure's criminal history. He said:

"The history and characteristics of the defendant (McClure), especially in your early years, as you point out, are — well, 'sordid' might be a word. I mean we have a couple of – we have the assault, the sexual component. But the one thing that — and neither counsel really addressed it but it's pretty obvious — is there appears to be this 10-year period with no additional offenses. That could be one of two things. You're very clever and you don't get caught, or you're being good."

Judge Clark then explained he didn't want to downplay the work of the government, but he just couldn't see the importance of pursuing this matter unless it was a situation like the Al Capone case in Chicago where it was the only possibility the government could put away a really bad guy.

He seemed to be unsure if McClure was the unwitting owner of guns who thought he could legally have them under state law, or was the person behind the drug trafficking and wiretapping revealed during the suppression hearing.

Judge Clark chose to give McClure the benefit of the doubt. Although the maximum sentence for felon in possession was 10 years, the United States Probation Office recommended a sentence of between 46-57 months. Judge Clark gave McClure what is called a downward departure and sentenced him below the recommendation — 36 months in prison.

In wrapping up the sentencing, Judge Clark reminded McClure that although he had very little chance of winning an appeal (as he basically gave up all his rights to appeal by pleading guilty), he had 14 days to give notice to the court if he planned to appeal.

McClure spoke up and said "Okay. Well, your Honor, so it'll be on the record, I do want to appeal."

He had plead guilty, been given a generous sentence, and yet smugly announced he planned to appeal. I began to believe McClure actually enjoyed being in court and being the center of attention. That belief only became stronger in the many subsequent court hearings I would attend on McClure issues, many of which were the result of motions he authored.

Ironically, those motions ultimately had the effect of keeping him in jail longer than he otherwise would have had to serve, if he had stuck with his initial cooperation.

After adjourning the sentencing, Judge Clark asked prosecutor Lisa Flournoy back to his chambers. Clark asked if there were more charges coming against McClure. He was worried he made the wrong decision in downward departing and was letting McClure off too easy. Flournoy assured the judge there would be additional charges and the gun possession case was a small matter that unexpectedly came up during the course of a larger investigation which was still ongoing.

After meeting with the judge, Flournoy told Blaine Gillis and I she planned to indict McClure and Walker for the drug trafficking associated with the theft of drugs from the Tenaha Marshal's Office in the grand jury in September. We planned to meet later and begin preparing. It was a meeting that wouldn't take place.

17

SUBSTITUTIONS

About two weeks after McClure's sentencing, Lisa Flournoy called me and said she was leaving the U. S. Attorney's Office to pursue private practice.

"It's an opportunity I just can't pass up," she said.

She planned on leaving in three months.

"Management doesn't want me to seek any indictments on my assigned cases until they're re-assigned to other prosecutors," she added.

I was happy for Lisa, but it would mean the indictment of Fred Walker and Rod McClure would likely be put off until the first part of 2013 so that a new Assistant U.S. Attorney could review the case.

The case was re-assigned to Greg Marchessault, an experienced prosecutor who was methodical in preparing a case for indictment. I knew Greg would thoroughly review the case, assess where the weak points were, and anticipate potential problems. I was confident he was an excellent choice to prosecute the case. The only problem was he was finishing up a temporary duty assignment out of the country and was not due to return for another six weeks.

I was pleasantly surprised, however, that when he returned from the temporary duty, Greg got up to speed very quickly on the case. I wasn't as pleased to learn that he was skeptical of proving Walker's involvement in the case.

Remember, we had a significant amount of evidence directly linking McClure to drug trafficking and the Marshal's Office burglary — text messages, photographs of marijuana at his home, significant and unexplained cash deposits in his bank account, direct testimony from Terrence Ford, Amy Johnson, Kenneth McCaney, and McClure's cellmate, Bobby Roy Bachman. In addition, we had two separate admissions from McClure himself.

Fred Walker, on the other hand, had only admitted to involvement in wiretapping the Marshal's Office and City Hall, and unfortunately, we found no incriminating electronic evidence in our analysis of the computers seized at McClure's home.

There were unexplained cash deposits in his bank account as well but they weren't as large as McClure's deposits.

There were the hundreds of phone calls between Walker and McClure. And although McClure had freely told Ford about Walker's involvement, it was hearsay and wouldn't be admissible in court.

Greg felt if we didn't have McClure's cooperation, which didn't seem to be forthcoming, we could not prove the case against Walker. Revealing and prosecuting the corruption by a law enforcement officer was the whole point of the case.

Another area that Greg found troubling was the involvement of Barry Washington as a key witness. Because Washington had been a defendant in the *Morrow vs. City of Tenaha* federal civil case and the target of the Department of Justice criminal investigation into the narcotics interdiction stops, Greg felt a good defense attorney could implicate Washington as being involved in wrongdoing.

Washington was important as a witness because in the drug trafficking case he had seized and placed in evidence most all of the drugs stolen from the Marshal's Office evidence room through the interdiction stops. He could help establish that the drugs had been stored in the evidence room.

Greg reasoned that although Washington had successfully testified in many federal drug cases during his career, the allegations in *Morrow* of racial profiling and heavy-handed police tactics could taint his credibility, even though those allegations had never been proven.

In addition, although he had not been charged with anything resulting from the DOJ investigation, Greg knew the DOJ prosecutors were skeptical about Washington's involvement. Even though it was only a perception issue, perception is everything when it comes to dealing with juries, and a good defense attorney could paint a bad perception.

In further evaluating the use of Barry Washington as a witness, Greg obtained a deposition Washington gave during the *Morrow* case. In that deposition, Washington stated his decision to go to work in Tenaha was made after a vision from God told him to go there. My opinion was if he believed he had a vision from God, he was probably being truthful about it. It would have been easy to leave the vision out in his testimony and explain it another way without directly invoking God. But the fact he said it anyway demonstrated a measure of sincerity to me.

Greg looked at it from the standpoint of the average juror, who might find the statement uncomfortable or off-putting. It would certainly be something a defense attorney could use to attack Washington on the stand.

So the decision was made: Washington would not be used as a witness.

We would have to use less direct testimony from other witnesses, but we would still be able to establish the narcotics stolen from the Marshal's Office had been placed there as evidence.

Another problem Greg spotted was a discrepancy between the texts and photos McClure sent to Terrence Ford listing the amounts of drugs he had and the missing drugs from the Marshal's Office evidence room.

Overall, the amounts McClure listed were close, although not exact, to the known amounts of stolen drugs. However, among the photos McClure sent to Ford was one of a bag of a white powdery substance. The accompanying text described it as nine kilos of cocaine.

This would be a significant amount of cocaine to be charged with and would greatly increase a potential sentence upon conviction. The discrepancy was that none of the missing evidence included cocaine. The only large seizure of cocaine Barry Washington made was accounted for and was appropriately handled by the Department of Public Safety.

This meant McClure was either lying about having cocaine in the text message or he was selling drugs from another source other than the Marshal's Office evidence room.

I suspected it was the latter, because the amounts and time period of the cash deposits in his bank account seemed to be greater than what he would have made just from the stolen narcotics.

It would be very difficult — if not impossible — at this point in the case to prove where McClure might have had another drug source. But we had him in his own words soliciting Terrence Ford to help him sell nine kilos of cocaine along with the marijuana and pills stolen from the Marshal's Office. So the nine kilos of cocaine were included in the indictment.

In September 2013, Rod McClure was finally indicted for drug trafficking associated with the theft of drugs from the Tenaha City Marshal's Office. Fred Walker was not named in the indictment, but was described as a "confederate" of McClure who helped him carry out the scheme.

The strategy of the United States Attorney's Office was to convict McClure on the drug charges and because he was facing such a significant amount of prison time — up to about 25 years — he would likely seek to cooperate and provide incriminating information about Walker to help reduce the sentence.

It was a reasonable strategy, given the circumstantial case we had against Walker.

The plan was based on McClure making a reasonable choice and it would have worked with the majority of defendants.

But by this point in the case, McClure had become confident in his legal knowledge and I believe he was actually enjoying the process.

——

In August 2013, ATF Agent Blaine Gillis and I learned of some information from a confidential informant that McClure was planning to kill Fred Walker. The informant had heard from McClure's cousin, "Buddy," that Rod was unhappy with Walker because Walker was slow in making payments to Rod.

The informant heard from Buddy that Walker had promised to pay Rod money for keeping quiet about Walker's illegal activity. Rod was apparently getting nervous that Walker wasn't going to pay and said the first thing he was going to do when he got out of prison was have Fred Walker killed.

The informant's information was credible to us because of an earlier recorded jail telephone call between McClure and his brother in March 2012. In that conversation, McClure said he had been promised $40,000 to keep his mouth shut while in jail:

"I was supposed to have been given $40,000 to keep my mouth shut about some tapes, do you understand? And now I'm losing my home, I have to sell my house and everything else and I haven't got my money and it pisses me off, do you hear me?"

This could explain why McClure had not cooperated. But after two years in jail, maybe McClure was realizing $40,000 wasn't that much.

Both Gillis and I felt we had a moral obligation to tell Fred Walker about the possible threat on his life. Prosecutor Greg Marchessault agreed.

We contacted Walker at a hospital in Nacogdoches, Texas where his elderly mother was being treated. We told him what we knew about the threat. With a slight laugh indicating to me he thought the information was ludicrous, Walker said he wasn't worried about it and he had nothing further to say.

I learned through a subsequent jail call that Walker immediately told McClure about our contacting him. McClure was incredulous that we would think he was involved in such a scheme, but if there was any credibility to the informant's information, I think we might just have saved Walker's life. McClure was smart enough to know that if something happened to Walker now, he would be the top suspect.

Not long after this, Greg Marchessault was chosen for another temporary duty assignment in Germany. It meant there would have to be another delay in the case for a new prosecutor to get up to speed.

The case was re-assigned to Jim Noble, another veteran prosecutor with experience in drug and gun cases. Jim prepared very quickly on the case but as it turned out he could have taken his time.

McClure could not find an attorney with whom he was satisfied. After being sentenced on the felon in possession case, he had apparently grown disillusioned with Lori Mack. He went through two lawyers — and a brief period of wanting to represent himself — before the attorney who ultimately represented him, Kelly Pace, was appointed. This process of changing lawyers would take months of hearings and delays.

18

NON-TAX RELATED CHARGES

While the delays associated with McClure's attorneys were dragging on, Gillis and I began looking into another scheme Walker and McClure were rumored to be involved in: Arson.

When Texas Ranger Tom Davis and I first interviewed McClure at his computer shop, we noticed he had a beautiful new home immediately adjacent to the computer shop. It was one of the nicest homes in Tenaha. It was built in 2008 to replace an older home that had been destroyed by fire in late 2007.

In our proffer interview of Terrence Ford he speculated that McClure burned down the original home, an older frame house, to collect insurance money.

"In the months before it happened, Rod had been talking about how much money he could collect if the house burned down," Ford said.

He told us after collecting the insurance proceeds, McClure not only built a new house significantly more expensive than the original, but paid to take him, Fred Walker and several others on a Caribbean cruise. When Ford told us this, we were focused on the drug trafficking case and didn't have the time or resources to look into it.

However, during a subsequent interview with Becky Sayles, the truck stop clerk who saw Walker loading a box into his patrol car at the Marshal's Office the night of the burglary, we learned of rumors she heard that McClure had burned his house down for insurance money, and that he later took several people to Mexico. Sayles said a man named John Cooks told her he had helped McClure burn the house down and was mad he wasn't taken on the trip to Mexico.

John Cooks' name would arise later when he was found dead of an apparent heart attack — on the same day David Thompson, McClure's friend being investigated for child pornography, was found dead from an apparent suicide. Both deaths were investigated by Fred Walker.

Another thing we learned was that Walker was also the town Fire Marshal who would have been responsible for calling in the state Fire Marshal to investigate the fire. However, that call wasn't made and the fire was ruled by Walker to be accidental.

Some preliminary work revealed the home that burned, an older and smaller frame house, was insured for almost three times its value.

I thought this might be an area where we could find some direct incriminating evidence of illegal activity against Walker. If the fire had been an arson that Walker helped officially cover up, as we believed he had done in helping stage the Marshal's Office burglary, it would be insurance fraud.

Even though it occurred five years earlier, fraud schemes against insurance companies, which are considered financial institutions, have a statute of limitations of 10 years.

When I presented this idea to the United States Attorney's Office, prosecutor Jim Noble felt it certainly could lead to Walker's involvement in the scheme but, like the drug trafficking case, it would require proving McClure's involvement as well.

Because we had so much already pending against McClure, Noble made the decision not to pursue the insurance fraud because it could appear we were unfairly piling charges on him.

—

Despite his misplaced self-confidence in defending himself in court, Rod McClure met his match in attorney Kelly Pace. During a preliminary meeting at the U.S. Attorney's Office shortly after he was appointed to represent McClure, I was impressed with Pace's grasp of the case and all its nuances and subtleties.

Although I don't know what was specifically discussed between McClure and his various attorneys during this case, I suspect the conversations went something like this: "Rod the government has a strong case against you. We can argue small technicalities, but we will likely lose those arguments. Your best strategy is to cooperate against Fred Walker, reveal any public corruption you know about and try to get the best deal you can."

Not wanting to hear that advice, McClure fired the attorneys.

In a hearing to appoint him a new attorney, United States Magistrate Judge John Love told McClure he could not keep firing attorneys because they weren't telling him what he wanted to hear. So now McClure would have to deal with Kelly Pace.

In the preliminary meeting, Pace acknowledged the evidence against McClure was overwhelming, but said he planned to seek a dismissal hearing to argue the drug trafficking case should be thrown out because of specific wording in the plea agreement in McClure's previous felon in possession case.

True to his word, Pace filed the motion and a hearing was held before United States District Judge Michael Schneider, the judge before whom McClure's trial on the drug trafficking indictment was scheduled to be held in October 2014.

Nearly a year after he had been indicted and on his third attorney, McClure had a hearing which would ultimately come down to the meaning of the word "related."

In what was actually a mini-trial, witnesses to be called were sworn in and then defense attorney Kelly Pace and prosecutor Jim Noble each made opening statements to Judge Schneider.

The crux of Pace's argument was the drug trafficking and the felon in possession cases were related, and therefore, language in the plea agreement of the felon in possession case would require that all "non-tax related" charges against him, i.e., drug trafficking charges, were to be dismissed.

Relying heavily on my search warrant affidavit in which I gave the entire background of what had been found in Tenaha, Pace argued it was one large case and the drug trafficking charges would have to be thrown out.

Prosecutor Jim Noble argued that the cases were not related, that is, the underlying conduct of having guns in his home — to which McClure pleaded guilty — that were discovered during a search warrant looking for evidence of illegal wiretapping was not related to a much larger multi-state drug trafficking conspiracy.

He said the meaning of non-tax related charges, which was standard language in a plea agreement, was that charges of the same nature as the charge to which a defendant was pleading guilty. He added it was unreasonable for McClure to conclude that charges involving a two-state ongoing drug conspiracy with a corrupt police officer would be considered related to his illegally having guns in his home. The only relation between the two was the involvement of McClure himself.

In an ironic twist, Kelly Pace called Lori Mack, the attorney who represented

McClure in the felon in possession case to testify it was her understanding that by pleading guilty, McClure would have the drug trafficking charges against him dropped.

During Mack's direct testimony she said, "In my talks with Mr. McClure and my advice with Mr. McClure, when we were in those plea negotiations... it was both our understanding that Tenaha (drug trafficking) was not going to be a part of that..."

Under cross examination however, Jim Noble was able to show she had no good basis on which to draw that conclusion as she acknowledged prosecutor Lisa Flournoy never actually said the drug trafficking charges would be dropped:

Q: Did Ms. Flournoy say that by pleading guilty to the guns in his home, Mr. McClure needn't fear further prosecution for his drug trafficking scheme?

A: She didn't say that specifically.

Q: Did she suggest to you that by pleading guilty, Mr. McClure would not have to face prosecution for his role in a drug trafficking scheme?

A: I don't recall specific sentences.

Also, during the cross examination, Noble questioned Mack about a letter McClure sent to Judge Ron Clark while awaiting sentencing on the felon in possession case. In the letter, McClure listed several complaints against Mack. He said she made false representations to him, had failed to visit him prior to the suppression hearing, failed to tell him of her previous license suspension and ignored his "bipolar disorder" in convincing him to plead guilty to the felon in possession charge. Noble questioned regarding McClure's allegations:

Q: Do you recall that he (McClure) complained about a medical condition prior to entering his plea of guilty?

A: Yes.

Q: And did you feel if affected his ability to enter a plea of guilty?

A: No.

Q: McClure says you told him that he should not trust the Federal Public Defender's Office because they want to help the United States Attorney's Office. Did you tell him that?

A: No.

Q: So that wouldn't be true?

A: No.

Q: And he (McClure) said that you told him that you had lots of experience doing federal criminal work. Did you tell him that?

A: No.

Q: And he also says that you told him that he would be out on bond in two weeks. Did you tell him that?

A: No.

Q: He (McClure) represents to the Judge that you said the Court was holding up your substitution (into the case) because the government did not want you to substitute in the case.

A: That's not true.

Q: He (McClure) said he informed you that he had been out of it mentally because he was given the wrong medication and that he was still suffering from the side effects of the wrong medication and he didn't think it was a good idea (to testify).

A: I recall him telling me that... he was taking medication... but he never informed me that it was not a good idea to testify.

Noble finished up the line of questioning with:

Q: Okay. So based on what you're telling us here today, Mr. McClure has made false representations to the Court about these things you told Mr. McClure?

A: Yes.

Because the defense had sought this hearing, they had the burden of proving McClure understood that all drug trafficking charges against him would be dropped at the time he pleaded guilty on the felon in possession case.

In just a few questions, Jim Noble had been able get McClure's own attorney to say he had lied in his letter to the Judge. This was devastating to the defense — either McClure was lying or his attorney was lying.

McClure did not take the stand and he was under no requirement to do so. But since the entire thrust of their argument was based on his understanding of the words "non-tax related charges," it would only make sense that he would testify. My opinion is he didn't want to face cross examination — but I never knew the real reason.

By leaving Mack's testimony that McClure made misrepresentations to

Judge Clark unchallenged, any credibility he might have had remaining was now completely gone.

McClure had written the letter complaining about Lori Mack in May 2012. In my opinion he probably wrote the letter in the hope that Judge Clark would simply throw out the case based on the egregious allegations against his own attorney. But in October 2014 that same letter was used against him. It was a perfect example of McClure's shortsighted tactical maneuvering coming back to haunt him.

Judge Schneider ruled against McClure and found the "non-tax related" language in McClure's felon in possession guilty plea did not include the subsequent drug trafficking charges. Thus, the drug trafficking case was set to go to trial in January 2015.

But McClure still had another card to play.

19

THE PROFFER

A couple of months after the failed dismissal hearing, McClure's attorney, Kelly Pace, contacted Jim Noble at the U.S. Attorney's Office and said McClure wanted to provide information through a proffer — a "queen for a day" session — ostensibly to provide information he knew about corruption. Maybe this was what we were waiting for.

But by this point McClure's credibility with us was gone.

"If McClure is going to roll over on Fred, I hope he has something we can corroborate because we can't trust anything based on his word alone," I told Blaine Gillis.

"I wouldn't hold your breath for that," Gillis responded.

Arrangements were made with the jail where McClure was being held. Blaine Gillis, Jim Noble and I met with Kelly Pace and McClure for the proffer. This time it was audio recorded. Although he didn't say it, I believe Pace was relieved when we told him the session would either be recorded or not take place at all. Kelly is a very smart guy who was dutifully and diligently working in the best interest of his client. He also must have reasoned that McClure would turn on him as easily as he had on Lori Mack — if he thought it could help him.

The proffer lasted about four hours. It wasn't what we hoped it would be. Essentially, McClure went through each witness we had in the case against him and made incriminating allegations, in an effort to proactively discredit and impeach each one before trial.

McClure had details on Terrence Ford regarding their days together as DEA informants. He alleged Ford had planned to kill a DEA Agent and was involved in the murder of a Tyler, Texas drug dealer in the mid-1990s.

He said that Kenneth McCaney was a hit man, and that current City Marshal Tom Reader was corrupt. McClure said his family had recordings of Reader attempting to bribe witnesses.

At one point during the proffer, I sarcastically said to McClure "It is so surprising with all this crime and mayhem going on around you, and Fred Walker's not involved in any of it."

I asked McClure about a series of letters that were mailed in 2009 to various Tenaha churches and businesses that contained extremely racist and violent language and images threatening Barry Washington. The letters had been analyzed for fingerprints with negative results. McClure claimed to have no knowledge of the letters.

Gillis and I were subsequently able to run down most all of McClure's allegations and found no substance to any of it.

We interviewed several people who McClure told us could confirm all the allegations against our witnesses. None of it amounted to anything. Certainly nothing that could be corroborated. One of his former DEA handlers recalled McClure couldn't be trusted and they had suspected he was dealing drugs while he was an informant.

The recording he claimed caught Tom Reader bribing witnesses ended up being about an hour of McClure's father talking to a mechanic about a vehicle repair and then driving to a Mexican restaurant where he ordered chips and hot sauce — but nothing concerning Reader.

McClure revealed two things, however, during the proffer that were of interest:

He was the original source of both the Anderson Cooper 360 story about the Barry Washington interdiction stops and the *Morrow vs. City of Tenaha* civil lawsuit, both of which had brought so much attention to Tenaha. This confirmed previous information I learned from the civil attorneys involved in the *Morrow* case that they were getting information from a anonymous source.

McClure said he reached out to the media and the civil lawyers because he felt Washington and the other officials were committing civil rights violations. I didn't believe him at all. I suspect he reached out thinking a civil lawsuit and very negative media attention would cause Washington to quit his job as Deputy City Marshal and move on.

With Washington gone, McClure would have had the full protection of Fred Walker against arrest or investigation of illegal activities. When it didn't work, they illegally wiretapped Washington in an effort to gain incriminating or compromising information, which also failed.

20

DAVID THOMPSON

One last thing McClure brought up during his proffer session was the 2010 death of David Thompson, his friend — with whom he had worked at the Tenaha Water Department and from whom he had learned to cook methamphetamine.

McClure said he wanted to quash any thoughts that he was involved in murder. He said people thought he had killed Thompson and he wanted it clear:

"I don't do murder," McClure said. "That can get a needle in your arm."

Hearing him say — and so emphatically — that he was afraid of the death penalty further convinced me that Thompson's death might be the reason the former DEA informant wasn't so ready to cooperate. This had to be the reason he was so steadfastly protecting Fred Walker — if he implicated Walker in drug trafficking, Walker might implicate him in Thompson's death and McClure was afraid of getting the death penalty.

McClure said Dan Ulman, someone he'd sold marijuana to over the years, had killed Thompson because Ulman was afraid Thompson would cooperate with the Secret Service, which was investigating him for child pornography. McClure of course had no hard evidence of this. He acknowledged it was only his suspicion.

But wasn't it convenient he could cast doubt on Ulman, who was going to be a witness against him at trial and throw suspicion off himself in Thompson's death?

Since McClure raised the issue of David Thompson's death, going so far to allege he was murdered by a witness we planned to use against him, Blaine Gillis and I began looking into the matter in depth.

Even though we had often heard rumors about Thompson's death not being a suicide, the priority of the investigation was the corruption of drug trafficking by a law enforcement officer. In addition, early on — after gaining his full cooperation — I questioned Terrence Ford about Thompson's death and he said McClure had never given any indications of killing or having Thompson killed. So the issue remained a sideline matter.

But over the course of the investigation, and in light of McClure's fanatical unwillingness to help himself by incriminating Fred Walker in the drug trafficking case, I came to believe they must have had a mutual involvement in something more legally perilous than illegal drugs. They had to be protecting each other.

I knew from his jail calls that McClure said he was promised $40,000 to keep his mouth shut. But he already had spent three years in jail and was facing significantly more time if convicted in the drug case. While a DEA informant in the 1990s, McClure's reputation among his handlers was that he would inform on his mother if it helped him. I also knew that Walker had been paying a good portion of McClure's legal bills. The source of his money for this was from the estate of a deceased uncle.

By 2015 however, most of that money was long gone. So McClure was facing a lengthy jail sentence, Walker was out of money and yet neither one would budge about wanting to cooperate. Was it David Thompson's suspicious death that was keeping Walker and McClure silent and the possibility of "getting a needle"?

I will let you, the reader, decide — but here are the facts we discovered:

David Thompson lived alone in a small house at 209 Waller Creek Drive in Tenaha. The home he lived in is located immediately behind and on the same property as 213 Waller Creek Drive. Thompson's niece, Caroline Moore[21] resided in a separate house on the same property.

Thompson was 57 at the time of his death, was homebound and received medical care from a home health agency, Texas Home Health. He was visited daily by a nurse. Prior to becoming homebound, Thompson worked at the City of Tenaha Water Department. This is where he met Rod McClure.

Despite poor health, we confirmed Thompson was involved in drugs, illegal machine guns and child pornography. The computer onto which he downloaded child pornography was set up by McClure. The computer's associated IP addresses came back as being registered to McClure. McClure confirmed to us that Thompson was into child pornography, but he adamantly

---

[21] Not her real name.

denied having any involvement himself, and indeed, other than setting up Thompson's computers, there was no indication he was.

In late 2009, as part of an ongoing investigation into child pornography, the United States Secret Service identified an IP address that was distributing child pornography. The IP address of the computer came back to Roderrete McClure at 213 Waller Creek Drive in Tenaha. The Secret Service then obtained a federal search warrant for that address.

On Thursday January 21, 2010, the Secret Service executed the search warrant. They initially went to the address where Thompson's niece, Caroline Moore, resided. Moore acknowledged an internet connection had been run from her home to Thompson's home, which was immediately adjacent on the same property.

Moore told them Thompson was something of a hermit, who surfed the internet day and night. As they had not anticipated the computer with incriminating pornography would be rigged up through a connection at a separate home, the Secret Service did not have authority to enter Thompson's home and would need consent from Thompson or get a search warrant to enter.

They made contact with him at the front door of his residence. Thompson quickly became angry and uncooperative and refused to give consent for his computer to be searched. The Secret Service agents then backed away and contacted an Assistant United States Attorney in Beaumont to get a search warrant for Thompson's home. As they agents waited outside Thompson's home, he yelled at them from a window and said he would give his consent.

During the delay when the Secret Service agents were trying to get a search warrant written for Thompson's home, he made three phone calls to McClure. In his proffer, McClure acknowledged Thompson called and wanted to know how to erase his computers. McClure said he told Thompson he would not help him. It was presumably after these calls that Thompson decided to consent to a search.

Since he couldn't get McClure to help him erase the computers and with the Agents just outside his home, Thompson must have reasoned it was only a matter of time before they got a search warrant and would seize the computer anyway.

Telephone records revealed McClure placed two phone calls to Fred Walker after hanging up with Thompson. McClure made no mention to us in the proffer meeting about why he contacted Walker.

After allowing the Secret Service agents into his home, Thompson submitted to an interview. He acknowledged downloading pornography but said if it was child pornography it would have been accidental. Thompson didn't implicate anyone else in involvement and made no mention of other criminal activity. He was advised that a forensic examination of his computer would be completed in a few days.

While the agents were at his home, Thompson called his home health nurse, Stephanie James[22] and told her not to come by that day because he had people at this house.

After the Secret Service left Thompson's home, his actions are unknown. McClure however was busy making phone calls. He made a total of seven calls to Walker during the remainder of the day. He also made five unanswered phone calls to Dan Ulman, the individual he claimed he suspected of killing Thompson.

The next day, Friday, January 22, 2010, Thompson was visited by his home health nurse, Stephanie James who arrived about noon. James described Thompson as being in a very good mood. She said he watched television as she prepared a meal for him. When she left for the day, at approximately 3 p.m., James said Thompson wished her a good weekend and said he would see her on Monday.

That same Friday, McClure woke up early, calling Sebastian Ewing, one of his dealers (described to us by Terrence Ford), at 7:55 a.m. His call patterns seemed to be about the same. He made 18 calls to Fred Walker over the course of the weekend, from Friday through Sunday. And three calls were made to Dan Ulman during that weekend.

On Monday, January 25, 2010, home health nurse Stephanie James arrived at Thompson's home sometime between noon and 12:30 p.m. She knocked but there was no answer. She could hear the sound of the television inside. After about 10 minutes of knocking, James went to a nearby convenience store. James saw Fred Walker eating lunch. She told him something wasn't right at David Thompson's house.

According to James, Walker made a call to Rod McClure, apparently to get Thompson's telephone number. Phone records show he then called Thompson's number at 12:53 p.m. but there was no answer. He hung up and called McClure back. James recalled McClure arriving at the convenience store shortly after Walker called him. Walker then told her he would go to Thompson's house to check on him.

Apparently, Walker didn't go directly to Thompson's home, because James

---

[22] Not her real name.

said she called her supervisor at Texas Home Health, Kate Collins[23] about the situation. Collins, who was in the area, went immediately to Thompson's home and Fred Walker wasn't there. Collins was also unable to get an answer from inside the home. She checked and all the doors and windows were locked. While she was waiting, Collins called Thompson's sister and next of kin, Rebecca O'Neal,[24] who lived in Nacogdoches, about a 40 minute drive away.

Sometime between 1:30 p.m. and 2 p.m., Walker arrived at Thompson's home, followed shortly by O'Neal and her husband. Walker told Collins he couldn't enter the home without having someone from Thompson's family present.

In his brief written report of the incident, Walker said he met O'Neal at the Tenaha City Hall to have her sign a civil waiver of liability. This would protect him from liability for damage done to the home if he had to break open a door or window.

In a situation involving a homebound individual who is not answering the door, minutes could be the difference between life and death.

It took at least an hour from the time he learned from Stephanie James that something might be wrong before Fred Walker responded and attempted entry into Thompson's home.

Was he that worried about the civil liability or did he know that Thompson was already dead?

According to Kate Collins, the home health supervisor, Walker insisted she make entry into the home with him — another fact Walker documented in his report. To ask a civilian to accompany him into a home is both highly unusual and extremely dangerous. An officer never knows exactly what he is going to confront when entering a home. In this case, the odds were it would be a health issue.

But it also had to be considered that Thompson had recently been the subject of a search warrant and was under investigation by the Secret Service. Any reasonable officer would have considered the possibility of a barricaded situation with a person contemplating suicide and wouldn't for a moment consider making entry with an untrained civilian.

So why did Fred Walker, who was concerned enough about the civil

---

[23] Not her real name.

[24] Not her real name.

liability of entering Thompson's home that he delayed entry for over an hour, not seem to consider the danger he may have been putting a civilian into by insisting she make entry with him?

Was he using Collins so she could be presented as an objective witness to make his subsequent conclusion that Thompson's death was a suicide believable? If so, then his plan may have backfired.

Walker's report of the incident, which was less than half a page, indicated that upon making entry with Collins, he observed Thompson's body lying on a bed with his head hanging over the side. Walker failed to mention whether the body was on its front or back. He reported blood on Thompson's face and the rear of his head but did not report seeing a gunshot wound.

Walker's report next said that he took 11 photographs of the scene. Those 11 photographs have never been found. In our interview with Walker in August 2011, he claimed they should have been in the Marshal's Office, but we were unable to locate them.

Walker next reported the arrival of the Justice of the Peace, Larry "Dude" Jones, who pronounced Thompson dead and ordered an autopsy to be conducted. He detailed showing Jones the location of a .32 caliber Kel Tec pistol which was on the floor "under the side of the bed." Walker stated that personnel from Mangum's Funeral Home in Center, Texas removed Thompson's body from the scene. He concluded the report with the two-word sentence "Investigation continues."

When Blaine Gillis and I interviewed Collins, her full description of the incident was largely consistent with what was in Walker's short report, with one huge difference: Collins said Thompson was lying on his back with his left arm hanging off the side of the bed. Walker omitted the detail of how Thompson was facing and said his head was hanging off the side rather than his left arm.

"Are you sure about that?" I asked.

"Oh yes," she said confidently.

I believed her.

Gillis and I both realized that discrepancy — how Thompson's body was positioned — was hugely important, because he had died from a contact gunshot wound to the right side of the head.

"How could Thompson's body have ended up on its back, with a gunshot wound to the right side of the head and the pistol lying under the bed to the left side of his body?" I asked Gillis.

"He couldn't have," Gillis said. "It would be impossible."

This information implied he either was holding the gun in his left hand — which even for a person of youthful flexibility would be uncomfortable in orienting a gun to the right side of the head — or the scene was staged.

We both realized that just as the Marshal's Office burglary was staged to divert attention from the theft of evidentiary narcotics, we were possibly dealing with a staged crime scene meant to look like a suicide. So we began tracking down anyone else who might have seen Thompson's body before it was moved.

According to both home health employees, Stephanie James and Kate Collins, there was a lot of confusion as to who actually entered Thompson's residence. James said she did not enter. In a subsequent interview with Thompson's sister, Rebecca O'Neal, we learned she had not entered the residence either.

We located an employee of Mangum's Funeral Home, Wesley Melton,[25] who removed Thompson's body from the scene. Melton also recalled that Thompson was lying on his back, on the bed, with his left arm hanging off the side just as Collins described.

Finally, Justice of the Peace Larry "Dude" Jones said Thompson was lying on his back and the left arm was hanging off the side. Jones also commented that the gun was on the floor slightly under the bed.

We had three independent witnesses who described David Thompson as lying on his back with his left arm hanging off the bed. In addition, I obtained the autopsy photos of Thompson. They showed him to have a large amount of caked blood on his face that came out of his nose and had dried in streaks running toward his ears.

The streaks running toward the ears would indicate that he was on his back when the heavy bleeding from the gunshot wound occurred. Also, the photos indicated a heavy amount of lividity in his back. Lividity occurs when blood pools in the body after death due to gravity causing the skin to have a purplish to blue or black color. That it was so heavily pooled in the back would also indicate he was on his back when he died.

Fred Walker's report of the incident was just one-half page in length. Half of it was spent on the details of how he learned Thompson wasn't answering the door, how he contacted relatives to ensure he would avoid civil liability for entering the residence, and how he actually made entry.

For comparison, in an unrelated FBI investigation involving health care fraud on which I assisted, the subject of the case committed suicide

---

[25] Not his real name.

after being charged with the crime. The Tyler Police Department conducted the investigation of the suicide. In addition to numerous photographs documenting the scene, the very detailed report of the incident was several pages and described specifically how the victim was situated, measurements of the location of the gun and how it was oriented relative to the victim.

The only details Walker provided about the scene were that Thompson was lying on a bed with his head hanging off the side, that he could see blood on Thompson's face and the rear of his head, and the pistol was under the side of the bed.

But Walker didn't detail which side of the bed Thompson's head was hanging from, which way the body was facing, or on which side the gun was lying. However, both home health nurses told us the bed was in a corner of the room with the head of the bed being flush in the corner and the right side completely against a wall.

So it would have been impossible for Thompson's head to be lying off the right side of the bed and for the gun to have ended up under the bed on the right side.

The reader should understand that with a contact gunshot wound to the head, even with the relatively small caliber .32 found at the scene, a person would almost instantly be rendered unconscious if not killed instantly. In addition to the bullet itself, at such close range, the person would also suffer the concussive effects of the blast of gases emitted from the gun when fired.

When someone gets shot in the movies, the victim gets lifted off the ground or thrown back several feet from the force of the bullet.

But it rarely happens that way in real life. Especially involving a shot to the head.

Because there would be almost instant loss of consciousness or death, the victim of a gunshot wound to the head, such as the one Thompson suffered, would simply crumple and go completely limp. There might be some momentary twitching but no large movement — in other words, Thompson could not have shot himself standing across the room, and then stumbled toward the bed and dropped gun before falling on the bed.

Therefore it would have been virtually impossible for Thompson to have shot himself just above the right ear, somehow end up on his back on the bed with just his left arm hanging off as the three independent witnesses said, and the gun end up slightly under the bed near his left hand. The hand holding the gun would have simply dropped limply. The gun itself would not have been wildly thrown about.

Where it landed would be determined by how he was positioned when he shot himself. If he had been lying down, for example, the gun would have still been on the bed — on the right side of his head — not on the floor under his left hand. An examination of the bed sheets could have given an indication of whether he had been lying down — there would have been gunshot residue — but if that examination took place, it wasn't documented in Walker's report.

Maybe it would have been possible Thompson was holding the gun in his left hand when the shot was fired. In my opinion this would have been near impossible. He was, at 275 pounds, about 100 pounds overweight for his height of 5'7," and in bad health. He would almost certainly have lacked the flexibility required to hold the gun to the right side of his head with his left hand.

It also would have required a great deal of effort just to get himself in such an awkward position. Why would Thompson have gone to such an effort?

Thompson's toxicology report from his autopsy revealed he was positive for caffeine, nicotine, diphenhydramine (Benadryl), and methamphetamine. None were reported in toxic or lethal amounts. One other interesting chemical found in Thompson's system was acetaminophen — a simple pain and fever reliever. If Thompson was so distraught about killing himself, would taking medicine for a headache or other minor pain have been much of a consideration?

21

THE ORIGINAL STAGED CRIME SCENE?

Based on the findings detailed here, I believe at a minimum David Thompson did not die in the position in which he was found. The relative location of the head wound on the right side of his head, being on his back, and the gun under the bed on his left side, implies that if he killed himself, someone would have had to put his body in the position it was in when observed by the three witnesses. But if he did commit suicide, why would someone bother to move his body?

Despite the denials, the people who appeared to benefit from Thompson's death were Rod McClure and Fred Walker. Thompson was under investigation by the Secret Service for child pornography. They had just seized a computer from Thompson's home with an IP address registered to McClure. Thompson knew of McClure's involvement in illegal drugs and guns. Any close inspection of McClure would quickly lead to Walker.

The Secret Service search warrant and Thompson's death occurred in January 2010.

Shortly after they broke into the Shelby County Constable's office in September 2009, McClure told Terrence Ford he planned to begin stealing evidentiary drugs from the Tenaha Marshal's Office with Fred Walker's help. So the theft of drugs was likely occurring at the same time the Secret Service executed the search warrant. If Thompson had knowledge of the scheme, it would have put both McClure and Walker in jeopardy of being caught, if he told what he knew to the Secret Service.

The suicide of a person accused of involvement in child pornography is not necessarily an uncommon occurrence. The shame that society puts on such a crime is psychologically difficult for many suspects to handle. Because the City Marshal's Office would have had primary jurisdiction, it meant City Marshal Fred Walker would conduct the suicide investigation. By deciding so quickly that Thompson's death was a suicide, and by conveniently misplacing the 11 photographs he reported taking of the scene, and writing a report with a minimum of details, Walker helped ensure any further investigation by the Secret Service would be unlikely or fruitless. He may have hoped they would close the case and move on.

And that is exactly what happened.

The Secret Service wiped the illegal files from the computer, returned it to Thompson's niece, and closed the case. This would have been perfectly normal procedure, because at the time, they had no reason to doubt Walker's conclusion that their suspect had committed suicide.

Seven months later, another crime scene would be staged at the Tenaha City Marshal's Office — the "burglary" of the evidence room. Had McClure and Walker carried out staging this crime scene because they had successfully staged a previous crime scene and gotten away with it?

Only in the case of David Thompson, there were no related photographs and text messages sent to Terrence Ford as there were from the Marshal's Office staged burglary.

I believe David Thompson's death is the reason Rod McClure resisted cooperating against Fred Walker. If he openly testified against Walker, it meant Walker could reveal what he knew about Thompson.

Their mutual protection held throughout this case — except when McClure made the admissions to us of Walker's involvement in drug trafficking associated with the stolen evidentiary narcotics during the search warrant at his home, and his transport to Beaumont for his initial appearance on the felon in possession charge.

I think these admissions were an example of McClure's short-sighted tactical thinking, meant to get him out of the moment, such as when he threw out the wiretapping allegations against Walker that inadvertently incriminated himself and led to his arrest.

Fred Walker did his part to protect McClure. On the occasions we interviewed him, he only acknowledged the illegal wiretapping but claimed ignorance about other illegal activity McClure may have been involved in. Our financial analysis revealed he paid $15,250 to McClure's father, $8,600 to McClure's wife, Betsy Smith, and $5,000 to an attorney who represented Betsy.

Jail calls revealed McClure wanted money from "Old Boy," his code name on the recorded calls for Walker, to be given to his father to pay attorney fees. McClure's tone in describing the arrangement gave no indication of doubt that Walker would pay. Did Walker pay a total of $28,850 to McClure out of generosity? Or was it to pay for McClure's silence while he was facing charges?

Something else was suspicious, as mentioned earlier: Orlando Padron lived in a trailer less than 400 yards through some woods from David Thompson's house. It would have been easy to get to Thompson's home through those woods with little risk of being seen — certainly a car parked at Padron's trailer wouldn't have caused anyone suspicion — especially if no one was around, or if it was at night.

On the same day David Thompson's body was found, another death occurred in Tenaha of an individual who McClure told us was a close friend of Thompson.

John Cooks was found dead in his truck at 7:50 p.m. on January 25, 2010, a little less than eight hours after Thompson was found dead. Cooks' death was also investigated by Fred Walker. An autopsy revealed Cooks was positive for alprazolam (Xanax) and THC, the active component of marijuana. The report concluded, however, that Cooks died of natural causes due to an enlarged heart. Cooks' body was embalmed prior to the autopsy, which may have affected the toxicology findings.

In his proffer, McClure said he saw Cooks earlier that day and he was very upset after hearing of Thompson's death. McClure denied any knowledge of foul play relating to Cooks' death. A witness we interviewed earlier in the case however, Becky Sayles, told us Cooks admitted to her he helped McClure burn his house down in 2007 to collect insurance money and was angered McClure had not taken him on a Caribbean cruise with several others.

Although not as suspicious as Thompson's death, the coincidence of Cooks dying on the same day — four days after a Secret Service investigation began that could have revealed way more illegal activity than child pornography — does add to the mystery.

EPILOGUE

In November 2015, Rod McClure was sentenced to 56 months in prison after he pleaded guilty in federal court to drug trafficking conspiracy charges. The guilty plea came about after negotiations between the United States Attorney's Office and McClure's attorney, Kelly Pace.

Fred Walker was an unindicted co-conspirator in the matter because ultimately, the case against him was circumstantial and McClure never testified against him. That decision was the sole discretion of the U.S. Attorney's Office based on their best evaluation of possible outcomes if Walker went to trial.

So I will let you decide whether justice was served. Rod McClure and Fred Walker had an organized drug network operating with almost no risk from law enforcement.

When Barry Washington came to Tenaha, McClure helped initiate a civil lawsuit and a media campaign to get rid of him. The lawsuit and the media attention then brought in the federal government. It looked like it was going to work — Barry Washington's reputation was destroyed in the media, he was entangled in a lawsuit and was a target of federal prosecutors. It was only a matter of time and things would be back to normal.

But it all changed when McClure was betrayed by a friend who tried to extort the profits from his illegal scheme, and the spotlight of that federal investigation he brought about ultimately came back on him.

In violent crimes, robberies, kidnappings and other such crimes, it is easy to identify the victims of those crimes. The government provides all kinds of resources to help victims of crime recover, and rightly so. In public corruption cases however, the victim is the public in general, not necessarily any single individual. In this case however, I believe there were specific victims. Barry Washington and Randy Whatley both had their public reputations greatly damaged. To a lesser extent, so did former DA Lynda Kay Russell and

Investigator Danny Green.

There wasn't an organized effort in Tenaha to steal money from minority drivers passing through, but that media perception endures. And it all happened because Rod McClure wanted to keep dealing drugs, protected by a corrupt cop.

I was never able to understand why Fred Walker sent me the Jack Frost letter to begin with. I know he and McClure believed it was a real extortion. But they both had to realize that what was in the letter about them stealing drugs from evidence would be looked into.

Also, they should have considered that only a small number of people would have known about the scheme detailed in the letter, and the perpetrator had to be one of their own. I believe Walker and McClure were so arrogant in their belief that their staging of the Marshal's Office burglary was the perfect crime, they reckoned that even if the FBI looked into it, they had covered their tracks so well it was unlikely anything would come back on them.

As of the date of this writing, McClure is incarcerated in federal prison and is continuing to appeal based on the argument he should have been absolved of all guilt for his involvement in stealing and selling stolen evidentiary narcotics because he pleaded guilty to a felon in possession charge.

He has made that same argument to a federal District Court Judge, a federal Magistrate Judge, and the 5th Circuit Court of Appeals. He has lost each time.

Interestingly enough, in his most recent brief to the 5th Circuit Court of Appeals, filed in July 2016, McClure through his latest attorney, Reeve Jackson, admitted to the scheme of stealing drugs from the Tenaha City Marshal's Office with Fred Walker for the purpose of reselling them.

In a section of the brief titled "Statement of the Case" it accurately describes the scheme. A portion of it says "Mr. McClure, along with the City Marshal of Tenaha, Texas, Fred Walker, began stealing drugs from the evidence room of the city marshal (office) for the purpose of reselling the same. Eventually the conspiracy grew to include a third person named Terrence Ford. Ultimately, the group decided they needed to cover up their actions after they began to fear that an audit of the evidence room may reveal what they had done. To accomplish this they staged a burglary, poorly, of the evidence room and attempted to make it appear as though a Mexican drug cartel had raided the evidence room and taken guns and drugs."

So why tell an appeals court the truth after all the legal wrangling, fighting and maneuvering? And after several years in jail when, if he had cooperated as he initially intended, and testified for us against a corrupt law enforcement officer, most likely getting a much lighter sentence? The reader's guess is as good as mine.

I think it was to avoid the consequences of the death of David Thompson — but it could be something else that only Rod McClure and Fred Walker know.

As I said earlier, there was nothing routine about this case.

As far as the case of David Thompson, like the case against Fred Walker, it too was circumstantial. No forensic evidence links anyone to his death. Walker conducted no tests at the time of his death for gunshot residue on his hands.

I had a meeting with Shelby County District Attorney Ken Florence regarding David Thompson. He acknowledged the suspicious facts surrounding Thompson's death.

"I think there are probably enough suspicious facts to get a grand jury to indict," he said. "But I don't think we'd have a chance of getting a conviction at trial."

I didn't disagree with him at all. So the matter officially remains a suicide.

Thompson's death most likely will remain a mystery.

Perhaps though, like the case of Bobby Frank Cherry, the Ku Klux Klansman I arrested in 2000 for the bombing deaths of four African-American girls at the 16th Street Baptist Church in Birmingham, Alabama on the day I was born in 1963, the truth usually finds its way to the light.

Not always, but sometimes, sometimes.

Left to right: Constable Randy Whatley, District Attorney Lynda K. Russell and Tenaha Deputy City Marshal Barry Washington. Washington's presence in Tenaha was a threat to a drug trafficking scheme that involved the Tenaha City Marshal.

ON THE JOB: An FBI agent talks on the phone outside the Troup Police Department on Friday. An eight-week probe ended in the arrest of the Troup police chief and an officer Thursday night. — Staff Photo By David Branch

A newspaper photograph of the author taken during an unrelated public corruption investigation.

Tenaha City Marshal Fred Walker.

Roderrete McClure.

Photographs of drugs stolen from the Tenaha City Marshal's Office evidence room texted to a cooperating witness from Rod McClure. These photos broke the case open.

One of the boxes left behind at the staged burglary of the Tenaha City Marshal's office. The label on the box, a Texas Department of Public Safety laboratory sticker, helped identify the exact amount and type of narcotics stolen.

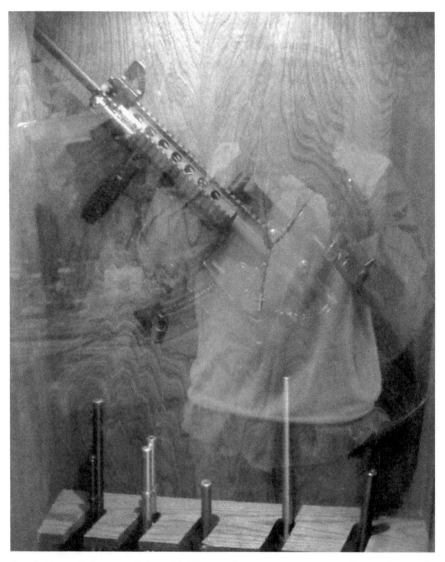

Another texted photograph from McClure to the cooperating witness that inadvertently captured McClure's reflection on the glass of the gun cabinet. The seizure of these guns unexpectedly gave McClure an argument that nearly derailed the case.

The cooperating witness' ineptitude at dealing drugs led him to attempt an extortion scheme against McClure and Walker because of texted photos like these from McClure bragging about his success as a drug dealer. Walker's referral of the extortion scheme to the FBI ultimately revealed the truth about corruption in Tenaha.

ABOUT THE AUTHOR

Stewart Fillmore retired from the FBI in 2016 after a 29 year career. He lives with his wife and family in East Texas. An avid tennis player, he enjoys playing guitar and tinkering on the banjo. He is currently the owner of a private investigation company.

CPSIA information can be obtained
at www.ICGtesting.com
Printed in the USA
BVHW01s1728110318
510289BV00010B/297/P

9 781547 248940